Celebration Bar Review

Georgia Essay Questions Book 2

This book is provided for the exclusive use of:

This Registered Celebration Bar Review Student

And may not be used by any other person without written permission of Celebration Bar Review. No Resale Permitted.

TABLE OF CONTENTS

FEBRUARY 2011 BAR EXAMINATION

QUESTION #1

In 1990, Abe graduated from the Medical College of Georgia, completed his residency training as a primary care physician, and became licensed to practice medicine in the State of Georgia. He decided to move back to his hometown of Climax, Georgia, and open a walk-in medical clinic.

Abe worked hard and prospered, opening clinics in nearby towns of Pelham, Coolidge, Iron City, Cairo, and Bainbridge, all in Georgia. Along the way, he took in a partner, Bob, and they formed a corporation named Climax Clinics, Inc. Abe owned 60% of the corporation and Bob owned 40%.

Upon the formation of the corporation in July 1995, Abe and Bob both signed shareholder agreements and employment agreements with Climax Clinics, Inc. The restrictive covenant in the employment agreement executed by Abe and Bob provided:

"Physician will not, directly or indirectly, alone or in conjunction with another person, practice medicine within a twenty-five (25) mile radius of a 'prohibited office' or see patients for consultation within a twenty-five (25) mile radius of a 'prohibited office'."

"'Prohibited office' is defined as one or more of the offices listed in Exhibit A to this agreement in which physician saw patients for Climax Clinics, Inc. within two (2) years of the date of termination of physician's employment with Climax Clinics, Inc."

Exhibit A to the employment agreement listed all the clinics which were open at the time of the incorporation. The exhibit had been amended to include all clinics opened by Climax Clinics, Inc. during the period of Bob's employment. Neither the exhibit nor any amendment thereto contained the specific address or location of any clinic.

The shareholder agreement executed by Abe and Bob with Climax Clinics, Inc. provided:

"The shareholders each covenant and agree that for two (2) years after a sale of shareholder's shares of the corporation, shareholder will not come directly or indirectly into the territory of any location at which the corporation is providing clinical services to provide professional services."

"'Territory' was defined in the agreement as 'that area within a fifty (50) mile radius of any Climax Clinics, Inc.'s clinic'."

As the business grew, the corporation employed several other doctors to practice in the various clinics. In August 2000, Chuck was employed by Climax Clinics, Inc. to practice in the clinic in Iron City. He and each of the newly employed doctors signed an employment agreement at the time of their employment with Climax Clinics, Inc. The contract which Chuck signed contained a restrictive covenant which provided:

"Physician agrees that upon termination of this agreement that he/she will not, for a period of five (5) years thereafter, within a fifty (50) mile radius of any Climax Clinics, Inc. clinic, engage in the practice of medicine in any capacity without the written consent of Climax Clinics, Inc."

In 2001, Abe and Bob had a falling out concerning the conduct of the business of the medical clinics, and Abe and Bob agreed that Abe would buy Bob's shares in Climax Clinics, Inc. Three (3) months after Bob's sale of shares to Abe and termination of his employment with Climax Clinics, Inc., Bob opened a medical clinic in Donalsonville, within twenty-five (25) miles of an existing clinic operated by Climax Clinics, Inc. in Iron City. Chuck was employed by Bob to practice medicine in the Donalsonville clinic with him. Abe believes that he can stop Bob and Chuck from practicing medicine in Donalsonville.

(1) To what extent, if any, is the restrictive covenant in the employment contract executed by Bob and Climax Clinics, Inc. enforceable?
(2) To what extent, if any, is the restrictive covenant in the shareholder agreement executed by Bob and Climax Clinics, Inc. enforceable?
(3) To what extent, if any, is the restrictive covenant in the employment agreement executed by Chuck enforceable?

NOTE: Discuss each covenant separately and fully, explaining the analysis to be used to determine the enforceability, vel non, of the agreement in question.

QUESTION #2

Bob and Betty began dating their freshmen year of college. By the end of their senior year, their relationship began to sour, and they decided to break things off. Bob graduated with a bachelor's degree and accepted an entry-level position with a large company, making a very handsome salary. Bob also purchased a home in a quiet residential area in Atlanta. Betty, on the other hand, could not find a job and moved back in with her parents, who also resided in Atlanta. Betty, who was once ambitious, lost interest in her previous career aspirations, refused to look for a job, and spent her days and nights lounging around her parents' home.

A month after graduation, Betty discovered that she was pregnant. While there is no dispute that Bob is the biological father of Betty's unborn child, she did not initially tell him about the pregnancy and wanted to conceal her pregnancy from him. Instead, Betty disclosed her pregnancy only to her parents and her best friend, Sue. Sue decided that she could not withhold this information from Bob and revealed the pregnancy to him.

When Bob found out about the pregnancy, he was furious. He confronted Betty, who admitted that she was pregnant, but she refused to discuss any of the details. Instead, Betty stated to Bob, "I don't want to have anything to do with you. I do not want any help from you. I am not interested in your opinions concerning this pregnancy. Leave me alone " On the day following this conversation with Betty, Bob comes to you seeking counsel concerning his rights.

Discuss what steps Bob should take under Georgia law in order to establish his rights as the legal father of Betty's child.

Assume for the following questions only that Bob is successful in establishing his rights as the father, is awarded full custody of the child by the Superior Court of Fulton County, Georgia, has lived with the child in Georgia since his birth, and has provided the child with a stable home environment, and by all accounts is a model father. Assume further that Betty's parental rights, however, were never terminated. Five years pass, and Betty has cleaned up her act, earned a graduate level degree and has landed a job that pays her a six-figure salary. Betty has purchased a new home in an upscale community and has established herself as a respectable member of the community.

Betty has not had contact with Bob or the child in over five years, but she contacts Bob expressing a desire to re-establish a relationship with their child, and advises him that she plans to seek custody of the child.

(1) What is the legal standard for making the custody determination?
(2) What factors must be established in considering the issue of custody?

QUESTION #3

Evergreen Nurseries is a greenhouse operation in south Georgia that grows produce seeds into seedling plants and sells the seedlings to growers.

Growers either tell Evergreen what type of seeds they want grown into seedlings and Evergreen buys the seeds, or the grower sends the seeds to Evergreen to grow them out. Once Evergreen has the seeds, it germinates the seeds in its greenhouses and grows them into seedlings. When the seedlings are ready to transplant, Evergreen sends the seedlings to the growers, who plant the seedlings as row crops and harvest produce such as peppers and melons.

Farm to Table, Inc. is a commercial pepper grower. At the beginning of this year's growing season, Farm to Table's office manager called Evergreen's sales manager and asked Evergreen to "grow some pepper plants for us for the fall planting season." Farm to Table's office manager confirmed the order with a fax to Evergreen. The fax stated:
This fax will confirm that we want to have 800 pepper plants for the fall growing season. We want seeds for 200 Stillettos and 200 Revolutions. We also want 400 Brigadier pepper plants. We are not sure how many seeds we will need for the Brigadiers. Please let us know how many Brigadier seeds we need to buy.

There was no other written confirmation of the transaction. Evergreen purchased the seeds for the Stilletto and Revolution peppers and advised Farm to Table that it needed to buy 600 Brigadier seeds. Farm to Table purchased the 600 Brigadier seeds from a seed dealer and had them sent directly to Evergreen by the dealer.

Evergreen invoiced Farm to Table, Inc. at the rate of $.028 for the Brigadier plants and $.063 for the Stilletto and Revolution plants. Although the rates for the Stilletto and Revolution plants included the costs of the seeds, this amount was not invoiced separately.

Shortly after the pepper seeds sprouted, Evergreen noticed that some of its Brigadier pepper plants appeared to be diseased. After samples were sent to the Experiment Station in Tifton, the plants tested positive for Bacterial Leaf Spot (BLS), a deadly plant bacterial infection. Once BLS is in the soil, it can reoccur in subsequent years, and Evergreen had had a BLS outbreak in the previous year. Evergreen attempted to halt the spread of the BLS in the Brigadier peppers by pulling the diseased plants and destroying them.

Evergreen shipped the remaining, apparently healthy, Brigadier plants to Farm to Table, Inc. However, a few days after Farm to Table's employees planted the Brigadier pepper plants, they also developed BLS and had to be destroyed. Subsequent tests revealed that Farm to Table, Inc.'s Brigadier plants were infected with the same strain of BLS as was found in the diseased plants in Evergreen's greenhouses. The Stilleto and Revolution plants sent by Evergreen to Farm to Table were not diseased, and Farm to Table had a successful fall pepper crop from those plants, but the Brigadier crop was a total loss.

Farm to Table, Inc. wants to file suit against Evergreen for strict liability, breach of warranty, and damages for lost profits from the loss of the Brigadier pepper plants.

You are an associate in the law firm hired to sue Evergreen. You are asked to provide a memo to the Partner in charge of the file on these issues:

(1) Can Farm to Table, Inc. bring a strict liability claim against Evergreen for the damages to the pepper plants caused by the BLS? Discuss the reasons for your answer.
(2) Can Farm to Table, Inc., bring a breach of warranty claim against Evergreen for the implied warranty of merchantability for the Brigadier plants? Does your answer change if the Stilleto and Revolution plants were the diseased plants and not the Brigadiers?
(3) What is the measure of damages for Farm to Table's loss of the Brigadier pepper crop and what must Farm to Table, Inc. offer as evidence to prove its claim?

QUESTION #4

Three new clients, Tom, Dick and Harry, have come to you for legal advice with respect to certain professional and business pursuits. All three are architects who wish to set up a new architectural firm in Athens, Georgia. They also have another acquaintance, Sally, who is in the real estate business but not an architect and who is interested in being a co-owner with them in the building of their office. All four have negotiated a construction loan from a local bank. The bank has said all four must personally guarantee the loan.

The architects need advice about what type of business entity or entities they should create for their professional practice and their office building. They are also concerned about possible malpractice claims, as well as any debts and liability claims which might arise from ownership of the building. They are willing to let Sally be the manager of the building, which could have some extra space to be rented to other parties until the architectural firm expands with more employees. The three clients have also said that Sally is willing to help them out by investing money in the architectural firm. The architects have also recruited a business manager whom they wish to be involved in the architectural firm as much as possible.

Given the choices of forming a common law partnership, a for profit corporation, a professional corporation, a tenancy in common, a limited partnership or a limited liability company, which would you advise the three architects as the best choice for their architectural practice under Georgia law? Briefly discuss the major benefits or limitations of these choices.

(1) What would be your advice for the best entity to own and operate the building? Why?

(2) Could Sally and their business manager own stock and be a member of the board of directors or an officer if they formed:

(a) A business corporation?
(b) A professional corporation?
(c) A limited liability company?
Why or why not?

(3) If the architects formed a professional corporation, what would happen to the stock of any shareholder who might leave the architectural practice for any reason, including death, assuming there is no written agreement on this matter?

(4) Assume the architects decide to form a professional corporation. What type of charter or other basic legal documents would you suggest they have and which, if any, of these documents would need to be filed as public documents with the Georgia Secretary of State or with the Clerk of the Superior Court of the county in which the principal office of the professional corporation will be located?

(5) Should any legal conflict arise among the three architects in the future, what should you tell them now regarding your role as legal counsel for any entity that you assist the three of them in creating versus your role as legal counsel for any or all of the three of them individually?

FEBRUARY 2011 BAR EXAMINATION ANSWERS

ANSWER TO QUESTION #1 (SAMPLE 1)

The employment agreement between Bob and Climax Inc. appears to be enforceable unless public policy preclude such restrictions upon physicians.

For a restrictive covenant in an employment agreement to be upheld, it must be limited in duration, scope, and geographic limitation. If the agreement is limited and not unduly burdensome, it will be upheld by the Georgia Courts. In the event the covenant tends to be a little too restrictive, GA courts may blue-pencil the covenant so that it can be complied with.

The covenant contained in the employment agreement is limited in duration because the time restricted is 2 years. Georgia has held that 2 years is a reasonable restriction. The agreement also limits Bob's ability to work during this time which is not excessive. However, there is an issue with the geographic scope of the covenant. The language of the Exhibit is not limited to particular addresses, so it gives the effect of precluding him from working in the town or any address within 25 miles of the town as opposed to the office. Therefore, Georgia courts may blue-pencil the restrictive covenant so that Bob is precluded from working within 25 miles of the office. (Unclear, but if public policy prohibits doctors from entering into restrictive covenant similar to the prohibition against lawyers to do so, the covenant will be enforceable).

For the reasons set forth above, the restrictive covenant in the employment agreement may need to be blue penciled by the court, but absent public policy, it is enforceable.

Shareholder agreements are agreements by and among the shareholder, the corporation, and the other shareholders. Such agreements list the duties and obligations of the shareholder to the other parties. Shareholder agreements may contain restrictive covenants.

The problem with the restrictive covenant in the shareholder agreement is that the term "Territory" is too broad. Territory is not defined as specific addresses, nor does it refer to facilities already owned and operated by Climax. Conceivably, Bob could comply with the terms of the restrictive covenant by providing professional services outside of the 50 mile radius, but if Climax later purchases a facility within the 50 miles radius, then Bob will be in breach of the covenant. Therefore, unless the GA courts blue pencil the geographic location to make it more specific the covenant is not enforceable.

Based upon the requirements set forth in Question 1, it is unlikely that a court will enforce the restrictive covenant against Chuck.

The restrictive covenant in this argument precludes Chuck, forces him to obtain the permission of his previous employer before he is able to accept new employment. Such a covenant is over burdensome in terms of the duration (5 years), geographic location (50 miles) and the requirement that he seek permission. The covenant essentially restricts Chuck's ability to obtain a living. Furthermore, Chuck is restricted from obtaining employment in areas outside of Iron City where he worked.

Even though Chuck is educated and not a lay person, there is significant unequal bargaining power that will likely preclude enforcement.

For these reasons, it is highly unlikely that a court will enforce the restrictive covenant against Chuck.

ANSWER TO QUESTION #1 (SAMPLE 2)

(1) As Abe is now the sole shareholder of Climax Clinics Inc., he is attempting to enforce the contract provisions against Bob. At issue is whether the restrictive covenant in the employment agreement is enforceable against Bob. Note that Georgia recently passed a constitutional amendment allowing for greater use of non-compete agreements.

Restrictions on employment are valid if they contain a limited duration, geographic scope, and type of employment prohibited. Non-compete agreements can be obtained from an employee in Georgia without additional consideration other than continued employment and are valid. The agreement states that Bob will not practice medicine or see patients within a 25 mile radius of a specific list of offices. Not including the addresses of the clinics will not be an issue as long as the prohibited locations can be ascertained and it is likely that it can be easy to find the locations of the offices. The prohibition is restricted to offices where Bob actually saw patients for the corporation within the past two years. This limits the prohibited areas to areas Bob recently worked. The problem with this covenant is that it does not provide a time limit. The agreement cannot prevent Bob from working in these areas forever and since courts tend to narrowly construe these provisions it will likely be held not enforceable.

Georgia has recently allowed "blue-penciling" of these agreements to allow the court to modify these agreements. It is unclear if the court would act to add a reasonable time frame to a non-compete that completely lacked such a provision.

(2) At issue is whether the restrictive covenant in the shareholder agreement is enforceable against Bob. Shareholder agreements can restrict the sales of shares, especially in a close corporation such as this where there are only two shareholders. Shareholder agreements may also contain non-compete restrictions and there is no issue of consideration because it is part of a bargained for exchange. The agreements still must be of reasonable scope and duration. This agreement attempts to be much more broad in its prohibited territories, prohibiting "shareholder from coming directly or indirectly into the territory of any location at which the corporation is providing clinical services to provide professional services." The agreement will likely be found to be too broad in that prevents Bob from participating in any market that the corporation's locations "providing clinical services." This definition of restricted territories includes locations that Bob has never practiced at and might expand to include more locations in the future and is too broad of a restriction on Bob. It also is not restrictive to the practice

of medicine as it prohibits any professional services which could include other professions. As the covenant defines the geographic scope too broadly, the courts will likely not enforce it as they narrowly construe non- compete agreements.

(3) At issue is whether the restrictive covenant in Chuck's employment agreement is enforceable. The non-compete agreement with Chuck provides a restriction on the duration of the agreement, 5 years. It also provides that he cannot compete within a 50 mile radius of any of the corporation's offices. This provision allows for consent to be obtained from the corporation which Abe appears not to be willing to give. Non-compete agreements can be obtained from an employee in Georgia without additional consideration other than continued employment and are valid.

This agreement, like the shareholder non-compete with Bob, lists all offices of the corporation as part of the restricted territory and therefore may be found too broad of a restriction to be enforced. As Chuck is working in Donalsonville, not Iron City where the Climax Clinic is located there is even less of a chance of the agreement being enforced.

ANSWER TO QUESTION #2 (SAMPLE 1)

1. Legitimation

Bob must file a legitimation action in the Superior Court of the county in which Betty resides to establish his legal rights to the minor child. In Georgia, a father has no legal rights to a minor child born out of wedlock. The only party with legal rights to a minor child born out of wedlock is the child's mother. A biological father, however, may request legal rights to his child by filing a Petition for Legitimation in the county of the mother and child. Bob will need to take immediate steps to protect his interest in the minor child because a putative father can abandon his opportunity interest in an illegitimate child.
As an initial matter, however, we are told that Betty is pregnant with the child. Because Bob has not yet been granted legal rights to the minor child, Betty could place the child for adoption without Bob's consent. Therefore, Bob should immediately register with the putative father's registry. The putative father's registry is a registry kept by the Department of Human Resources reflecting putative father that assert that they are the biological father of a minor child. Bob will want to register because he will receive notification if Betty puts the minor child up for adoption upon birth of the child.
By filing a Petition for Legitimation in the Superior Court, Bob will assert that he is the biological father of the child, that he has intimate relations with the mother, and he is a fit and proper parent to have legal custody of the child. Bob may also file for temporary and permanent custody of the minor child and seek parenting time in the same petition. The law in Georgia previously required that a minor child be declared legitimate before a biological and legal father could be awarded temporary or permanent custody of the child with a right of parenting time. That law, however, has changed and now a biological father can seek physical custody and the right of parenting time in the same petition.
Further, Bob will want to begin setting aside child support for the minor child. Bob will want to take this step even though the child is not born. Bob earns a "very handsome salary" and should begin putting aside child support, into the registry of the court or a

savings account, if the child is not yet born. Bob should take this step so that he can assure the judge in the Superior Court case that he is a fit and proper parent to have custody of the minor child. This is also a means for Bob to establish that he has not abandoned his opportunity interest in the minor child, whether born yet or not. A biological father has a constitutional right to establish legal rights to a minor child. However, a biological father can lose the right if he is not timely in pursuing his opportunity interest in the minor child. There are several ways in which a biological father may abandon his opportunity interest: by failing to provide child support, by waiting too long to seek to legitimate the child, and by failing to establish a familial relationship with the child.

Because Bob desires to protect his rights in the minor child, he should take immediate steps to protect himself and the child, including the filing of a legitimation action.

2. Child Custody Modification

Betty will be unsuccessful in modifying custody for two reasons. First, Betty cannot meet the legal standard. Second, an application of custody factors does not assist Betty in her quest for a modification of child custody.

A. Legal Standard

In an initial child custody case, a trial court applies the best interest of the child standard. However, in a child custody modification action, the non- moving party must establish that there has been a material and substantial change in circumstances that adversely affect the minor child. The change in circumstances cannot be that the non-custodial parent is now doing well. Instead, the focus is on the minor child and whether or not there has been a material and substantial change in circumstances adversely affecting the welfare of the minor child since the entry of the final custody order.

Here, five years have passed since Bob was awarded custody of the minor child. Betty is now doing well having "cleaned up her act." Betty owns her own home, completed a graduate level degree, and has landed a job that pays her a six-figure salary. While it is commendable that Betty is now stable, the trial court will focus on the minor child in making a determination as to whether or not to modify custody from the custodial parent to the non-custodial parent. We are not given any facts to assume that Bob has not been meeting the needs of the child or that there has been a material and substantial change in circumstances adversely affecting the welfare of the child. Therefore, assuming that Bob is stable and has been doing an excellent job of raising the child, Betty will not be successful in her child custody modification attempt. Because we are not given facts to assume that Bob has not been taking care of the child, it is likely that Betty cannot meet her burden of establishing a material and substantial change in circumstances affecting the welfare of the child.

B. Factors for Determining Custody

In an initial child custody determination, a trial court considers many factors, including the best interest of the minor child. In a child custody modification, however, there is a rebuttable presumption that arises that the custodial parent is the appropriate and fit parent to have custody of the child. The non-custodial parent must overcome the presumption.

Specifically, a final child custody order is conclusive between the parents and the non-custodial parent must prove that there has been a material and substantial circumstance adversely affecting the welfare of the minor child. The trial court will consider factors such as the child's ties to the community, the child's relationship with either parent, the ability of each parent to foster a relationship between the child and the non-custodial parent and extended family. Further, a trial court looks to how well the child is doing in her current custodial arrangement and if there has been a material and substantial change in circumstances since the entry of the final custody order. Because we are not given facts showing that Bob has not been meeting the needs of the child, it is unlikely that Betty will prevail.

ANSWER TO QUESTION #2 (SAMPLE 2)

1) The first step Bob should take is to register with the Putative Father Registry. This will have the effect of protecting his rights somewhat by requiring that he be provided notice of any action which would operate to his terminate parental rights or if Betty takes any other steps that would affect his rights before he can get before the court.

Bob may then file a Petition for Legitimacy with the Superior Court and submit evidence of paternity by way of DNA testing. A DNA test establishing at least a 97% probability of paternity gives rise to a presumption of paternity. Assuming this will be no problem for Bob to satisfy, proof of paternity will give rise to Bob's rights as a father notwithstanding that the child was born out of wedlock. Unless determined unfit as a parent, Bob has constitutional fundamental rights in the upbringing and education of his child. He may move for the court to award him custody of the child and/or visitation (if primary custody is granted to Betty – although the "tender years" doctrine has been abolished, there is still a presumption in favor of the child remaining with the primary caretaker as such is typically in the best interests of the child).

(2a) In all matters involving children, the controlling standard is "the best interests of the child." Although Georgia no longer recognizes the "tender years" doctrine, there is a presumption that it is in the best interests of the child to be in the custody of the primary care giver. In this instance, the facts suggest that Bob has been the primary care giver of the child for more than five years. As a custody order has already been entered, Betty will have to make a showing of "substantial change of circumstances" in order for the court to revisit the award of custody. However, such a showing will not be required for the court to modify to permit Betty visitation without making any change as to the award of custody of the child. Of note, because this matter is not multi-jurisdictional in nature, the UCCJEA (Uniform Child Custody Jurisdiction and Enforcement Act) does not come into play.

(2b) As noted above, to amend the order granting Bob custody of the child, Betty must show a "substantial change in circumstances." Arguably, such exists in this case – Betty has earned a graduate degree, obtained a well- paying job, purchased a new home, and has otherwise pulled herself together to become an upstanding and contributing member of society. Additionally however, the court will consider, above all, the best interests of the child. There is no indication of any questionable activities by either Betty or Bob that would potentially harm the child's physical, mental, emotional or moral health. In fact the only factor Betty has to raise is her recent change in circumstances as noted above. Because Bob has provided a stable environment for the child for the past five years and has by all accounts been a model father, the court may well find that it is not in the best interests of the child to remove him from his home to live with his mother. Factors considered will also include whether a change would disrupt the child's education, social or emotional ties. Since the child is under 14, there is no presumption in favor of granting custody based on the child's election. Much more likely an outcome is that the court would award Betty visitation (if she did not already have visitation) or additional visitation.

ANSWER TO QUESTION #2 (SAMPLE 3)

1. The issue is how is Bob able to legitimize Betty's child.

When legitimizing a child, the state of Georgia requires that the father petition the court. The alleged father will file a claim in the Superior Court in the county where the mother resides since this court has jurisdiction over these issues. The father will file a complaint with the court and have it served on the mother by a sheriff within 5 days of the filing of the complaint. The service should be to her personally or at her home to a person of suitable age. The mother will have 30 days in which to respond to the complaint with an answer.

The process of legitimization may include the review of a putative father registry and/or the performance of a paternity test. The putative father's registry is a device designed by the state to document the names of fathers who were engaged in sexual intercourse with a woman at a particular time in the event that a custody issue arises and they want to be contacted to ensure their rights to the child are protected. This registry is helpful in establishing preliminary rights of a putative father, but they are not conclusive without a paternity test. A paternity test is performed to test biological traits such as DNA of the father and compare it to the child. In the event that the DNA matches, the court will legitimize the child and grant the father legal rights to the child.

2a. The legal standard for making the custody determination is the "Best Interests of the Child".

In this case, the best interests of the child would be the continuity of their lives at home, at school and in their community. The child in this case has been with Bob for his entire life (five years) and has had no contact with his mother over that period of time. The facts provide that he is living in stable home environment and is living comfortably with Bob with his secure salary and his nice home in a quiet neighborhood. He is five years old and is most likely about to attend kindergarten. Even though Betty has finally gotten her life back on track, it may be a challenge to permit her to disrupt the continuity that has been established for the child over the last five years.

Since Betty's parental rights have not been terminated, it is possible for her to request custody of the child. In Georgia, no contact with your child for over a year is enough to establish abandonment. Therefore, her absence and lack of contact with the child for over five years would establish grounds for Bob to initiate termination of Betty's parental rights.

2b. The issue is what factors should be established in considering the issue of custody.

Custody can be determined by the best interests of the child by considering:
1. Parents' wishes
2. Child's wishes
3. Parents' ability to provide adequately for the child
4. Child's stability at home, school and community

In this case, both parents want custody of the child. Since neither of the parents' rights have been terminated and they both appear to be fit parents, it is very likely that they have strong arguments for raising a custody issue in court. However, as mentioned above, termination of parental rights can be petitioned if the moving party can establish that the non-moving party has abandoned their child and is not fit to care for the child. In this case, both parents appear to be fit, however Betty has clearly abandoned the child by not maintaining contact with Bob and the child for over five years.

In Georgia, a child between the age of 11 and 13 has persuasion over a judge's decision regarding custody. If a child over the age of 14, the judge will defer to the decision the child makes unless the parent is unfit and it is not in their best interest to be with that parent. In this case, the child is only 5 years old therefore, the child's decision is irrelevant and their best interests will be considered and determined by the court.

In this case, both parents appear to be able to adequately provide for the child. Bob has been employed at his job for over five years and makes a decent salary. He also owns a home in a nice neighborhood in Atlanta, where he has raised his child since his birth and conducts himself as a model father. Betty, on the other hand, has recently obtained employment paying six figures and lives in an upscale community. It appears that she would be able to provide the child with adequate provisions as well.

However, since both parents have maintained their parental rights and are both able to provide for the child, the best interests of the child will probably be determined by the stability of the child's home, school and community. It is possible that the best interests of the child could be met by allowing Betty some form of custody of the child, but it would definitely have an effect on the stability of the home, school and community that the child has established over the last five years with Bob. If Bob does not raise the termination of Betty's parental rights, Betty would be entitled to fight for custody of the child. The court could take all the issues into consideration and make the determination based on the best interest of the child at the time.

Additionally, in Georgia, child custody can be modified if a material change takes place. The parent wanting to modify the custody order would petition the court to modify custody and the court would take all the aforementioned factors into consideration at the time of modification and custody could be adjusted accordingly.

ANSWER TO QUESTION #3 (SAMPLE 1)

The issue is whether Farm to Table can bring a strict liability claim against Evergreen for the damages to the pepper plants caused by the BLS. Under Georgia law, a claim based on strict products liability may only be asserted against the manufacturer of the goods in question. While Evergreen germinated the brigadier seeds in its greenhouse, it received these from Farm to Table. In turn, Farm to Table had purchased the seeds from a seed dealer before having them sent to Evergreen directly by the seed dealer. In this context, Evergreen is not a manufacturer of the brigadier plants because the seeds were not grown by them. Instead, Farm to Table should pursue a claim of damages against Evergreen based on a negligence theory based on their breach of duty regarding the BLS-infected pepper plants.

The issue is whether Farm to Table can bring a breach of warranty claim against Evergreen for the implied warranty of merchantability for the Brigadier plants. A claim under the implied warranty of merchantability can be raised against a commercial supplier of goods of a certain kind. Evergreen is not a commercial supplier of brigadier seeds, as evidenced by the fact that Farm to Table had a seed dealer ship the seed to Evergreen. In this case, Evergreen merely provided a service whereby they take their customer's seeds and grow them into seedlings. As such, Farm to Table cannot successfully pursue a claim based on the implied warranty of merchantability against Evergreen for the diseased Brigadier plants.

If the Stilleto and revolution plants were diseased instead of the Brigadier, then Farm to Table could make a claim for the implied warranty of merchantability. Evergreen purchased these seeds itself in order to grow them into seedlings, which makes them a seller of such goods. Therefore, the implied warranty of merchantability would apply if the stilletos and revolutions were diseased.

Farm to Table should be awarded expectation damages for its loss of the full benefit of its contract with Evergreen. Under Georgia contract law, expectation damages are designed to put the non-breaching party in the position it would have been in had the contract been performed to its terms. To do so, he must offer evidence of how much his sales were hurt based on the unavailability of the pepper plants. He must present evidence of how much brigadier plants were selling for this fall, and he should be awarded that amount of his lost profits. He may also offer evidence of past-year's sales of brigadier plants to indicate how badly his full sales were offered due to the total loss of the brigadier crops.

ANSWER TO QUESTION #3 (SAMPLE 2)

MEMORANDUM
TO: Partner FROM: Applicant
DATE: February 22, 2011
RE: Farm to Table v. Evergreen

Farm to Table may bring a strict liability claim against Evergreen for the damages to the pepper plants caused by Bacterial Leaf Spot (BLS), but it is likely it would be unsuccessful. Strict liability claims are generally negligence claims reserved for when a party is engaging in inherently dangerous activities such as keeping wild animals for pets, for products liability claims or if legislation deems it a "strict liability" claim. Here, it is clear that raising plants is not an inherently dangerous activity.

Nor does Farm to Table have a products liability claim against Evergreen. To prove a products liability claim, they would have to prove that the product came from Evergreen, the merchant, which it did not. They would have to prove that it had a manufacturing or design defect, which is impossible for a plant. A products liability claim would not survive a motion for summary judgment out of the gate.

If Farm to Table brought a breach of warranty claim against Evergreen for the implied warranty of merchantability for the Brigadier plants, it would likely be unsuccessful. Under the UCC Article 2, a merchant, who is defined as someone who sells goods of a kind, issues a warranty with the goods they sell. These warranties can be express or implied. An express warranty is one that is expressly written into the contract. An implied warranty is one that is implied in the sale of the goods basically acknowledging that the product the purchaser is buying is guaranteed by the merchant.

Here, Farm to Table does not have claim for breach of implied warranty of merchantability because they did not purchase the Brigadier seedlings from Evergreen. Rather, they bought the seedlings from another merchant and sent them to Evergreen. Evergreen then provided them the service of growing the seedlings into plants. Because they were providing a service instead of a good, there was no implied warranty of merchantability for the Brigadier.

However, should the Stilleto and Revolution plants have been diseased as well or instead of the Brigadier plants, Farm to Table would have likely had claim for implied warranty of merchantability. These two plants were purchased as seeds from Evergreen, and therefore fall under the goods category. The other part of the contract was for Evergreen to raise the plants, which as discussed above, is a service. Because both goods and services are the purpose of the contract, it would be up to the court to determine whether the contract qualified mostly as a "goods" contract or a "services" contract in determining whether an implied warranty of merchantability claim exists.

The amount of damages for the loss of Brigadier pepper crop by Farm to Table can be measured in two ways: either by the amount it cost Farm to Table to replace the pepper crop plus incidentals, or their lost profits by not having the Brigadier pepper plant. To prove its damages claim, Farm to Table will likely have to provide the copy of the report sent back from the lab stating the Brigadiers were diseased, but not only diseased, but that the actual cause of the disease was the same strand from that at Evergreen. Additionally, Farm to Table will also need to provide an invoice to prove how much they paid to replace the diseased pepper plants. Or, if they could not replace the plants with others on the market, they would have to prove their lost profits. They could probably prove lost profits by showing how many orders they had for Brigadier pepper plants and what the likely profit would have been for the sale of those plants.

ANSWER TO QUESTION #3 (SAMPLE 3)

(1) The issue here is whether Farm to Table can seek strict liability damages, presumably

under a theory of liability for a defective product. Georgia law permits recovery under a products liability action only against the "manufacturer" of the product (and in some cases against the manufacturer of a specific component), and not ordinarily against a distributor, seller or other intermediary (unlike many other jurisdictions that permit recovery in these actions all the way up the chain of control). The issue here is whether or not in the unique context of these seedlings, Evergreen can be considered the "manufacturer" of the defective product (in this case the diseased plants), or whether Evergreen was merely an intermediary service provider. The facts provide that Farm to Table actually purchased the offending Brigadier seeds from a "seed dealer" and then had the seeds sent from the dealer to Evergreen directly, so that Evergreen could grow the sprouts.

Of importance here, Article II of the Uniform Commercial Code ("UCC") governs the sale of goods, which pursuant to the UCC includes seeds and crops. However, with respect to the Brigadier seeds, the facts indicate that these seeds were actually sold to Farm to Table directly, and were not purchased from Evergreen. Rather, with respect to these particular seeds, Evergreen was providing services associated with the initial planting (not goods). Because Evergreen did not actually sell the goods (i.e. the seeds) to Farm to Table, it would be inappropriate for the court to award any type of strict liability damages to Farm to Table based on a theory of products liability or otherwise. After all, with respect to these particular plants, Evergreen was providing services, not goods. It is worth noting that Farm to Table could contend that this is an indivisible contract that is primarily for goods (as opposed to services), based on the fact that the amounts for the various seeds and sprouts (the latter of which required services and not the sale of goods) were not invoiced separately. However, this theory is likely to fail based on the clear fact that with respect to the damages alleged, Evergreen was providing only services, and not goods.

(2) No, this type of warranty claim would not be appropriate with respect to the Brigadier plants. Pursuant to Article II of the UCC, a merchant (as defined in the UCC), in addition to any express warranties that it may give, is deemed to give an implied warranty of merchantability with respect to its goods sold. A warranty of merchantability is a warranty by the merchant that the goods being sold are fit for their ordinary use. However, in order for the warranty of merchantability to apply in this scenario, Farm to Table must demonstrate that the Brigadier plants were goods purchased from Evergreen such that Article II of the UCC would apply (thereby giving rise to the implied warranty of merchantability). As discussed in Section 1, supra, this is problematic, because Farm to Table purchased the Brigadier seeds directly from a seed dealer and then drop shipped the seeds to Evergreen for planting and sprouting. Of critical importance, there is no evidence showing that Evergreen provided anything other than services with respect to the Brigadier plants. Again, as stated in Section 1, supra, Farm to Table could claim that the entirety of its order was predominately an order for "goods" and is therefore governed by the UCC (supported by the claim that the goods and services were not separately itemized), but this theory is unlikely to be successful.

This answer would change completely in the event that it were the Stiletto and Revolution plants that contracted the disease and caused the damage, because with respect to the Stiletto and Revolution plants, the facts are clear that Evergreen provided the seeds, which would seem to create a viable claim that the sale of these particular plants was a sale of goods and therefore governed by Article II of the UCC. In the event that this were found to be the case, the implied warranty of merchantability would attach and Farm to Table would have a more viable claim against Evergreen.

The measure of damages for Farm to Table's loss is likely to be based on contract. Certainly, Farm to Table will be able to recover the amounts paid to Evergreen for the diseased plants, assuming that Evergreen cannot make a showing that the source of the disease was within the seeds themselves, which were provided to Evergreen by the seed dealer that was selected by Farm to Table. Generally, loss profits and consequential damages are not available to parties in contract unless specifically provided for in an agreement between the parties. However, under this fact pattern it is possible that Evergreen could have liability beyond a mere breach of contract, and could have tort liability for general negligence. In this case, it is possible that Farm to Table could recover lost profits stemming from the ruined crops. In order to recover lost profits, Farm to Table's claims cannot be merely speculative, but must be reasonably ascertainable. If Farm to Table can provide particular and specific evidence as to lost profits, it is possible that it could make such a recovery under Georgia law.

ANSWER TO QUESTION #4 (SAMPLE 1)

Business Form

Common Law Partnership – This is the simplest business form and it requires no filing or formalities. Also, taxes are on a pass-through basis to the partners. The major disadvantage is that all of the partners are personally liable for any debts of the partnership. Also, the partnership ceases to exist with the death of a partner or the removal of a partner.

For Profit Corporation A corporation is the most sophisticated corporate form. It requires filing for creation and following formalities to protect its limited liability status. (Formalities include creation of bylaws, election of president, secretary, and treasurer, taking of minutes at meetings, holding an annual meeting, etc.) A disadvantage is that double taxation exists on the corporation's profits. The main advantage is limited liability and the ability to have multiple classes of stock. To form a corporation, articles of incorporation must be filed with the Secretary of State. The articles must include the corporation's name and purpose, the names and addresses of the members of the corporation, the name and address of the agent of the corporation, and the classes of stock and the number of shares. A corporation survives the death or replacement of members. (continual existence)

Professional Corporation – A professional corporation is a form of corporation that can only be made up of people licensed to practice a certain profession. Formation requires filing as detailed above under "For Profit Corporation." The advantage of a professional corporation is that no one who is not a member of the profession can obtain ownership. Another advantage is limited liability and continual existence.

Tenancy in Common – Tenancy in common is a way to hold a deed to real property. A tenant in common can sell or borrow against his share of the tenancy. Unlike Joint

Tenancy where when one tenant dies, the other tenants automatically take the dead tenants share, a tenant in common can devise their share of the property. There is no liability protection for tenants in common.

Limited Partnership – A limited partnership allows limited liability to all limited partners. It requires filing and following of formalities. However, a general partner must be present and they do not enjoy limited liability. (In practice, the general partner is typically a corporation that already has limited liability.) The limited partners cannot actively manager the partnership. An LP has continual existence so long as one general partner remains.

Limited Liability Company – An LLC can be thought of as a lite corporation. It allows all members limited liability and requires filing and following of formalities. It also allows for pass through taxation. However, an LLC can only have one class of stock. An LLC has continual existence.

Best Choice: The best choice for the practice would be the professional corporation or the LLC. Both have limited liability protection and continual existence. The professional corporation has the advantage of limiting ownership to **only** architects. The LLC is a simple corporate form that allows flexibility and ease of pass through taxation that avoids the double taxation of the full corporation form. The LLC could allow the architects to allow non-architects to have equity ownership in the firm. The choice of form will be governed by whether the architects want to allow non- architects equity ownership. If so, an LLC is the best choice. If not a PC will be best.

Building
I would advise an LLC be created to own and manage the building. The LLC would allow the LLC shareholders to apportion ownership any way they saw fit. (Based on contribution or any other measure.) The LLC would also grant limited liability protection to the shareholders which is critical if the building will be rented to other entities. Lastly, the LLC would provide for pass through taxation which would simplify taxes and reduce the amount of taxes paid. (Avoids double taxation of the Corporation form.) The LLC would allow both architects and non-architects to own a share of the building.

Sally and Business Manager could own stock and be on board or an Officer

Corporation – Sally and the Business Manager could own stock and be on the board. There is no restriction based on occupation. The bylaws of the corporation may place some restrictions on who can be board members and officers. Generally the shareholders elect the board members at an annual meeting, and the board appoints the officers.

Professional Corporation – Sally and the Business manager could not own stock unless they were an architect. They could be an officer and serve on the board, however, they would have to excuse themselves from any decision that required an architect's license. The bylaws of the professional corporation may place some restrictions on who can be board members and officers. Generally the shareholders elect the board members at an annual meeting, and the board appoints the officers.

Limited Liability Company – Sally and the Business Manager could own stock and be on the board. There is no restriction based on occupation. The bylaws of the LLC may place some restrictions on who can be board members and officers. Generally the shareholders elect the board members at an annual meeting, and the board appoints the officers.

Professional Corporation – Stock on leaving or death

Since only members of a specific profession can own stock in a professional corporation, any member leaving or the estate of a dead member would have to receive the cash value of the stock they owned. This value could be calculated based on the bylaws or based on a valuation of the company performed by an appraiser.

Filing

To form a PC, the architects would need to file the articles of incorporation with the Secretary of State. The articles would need to contain the corporation's name and purpose, the names and addresses of the members of the corporation, the name and address of the agent of the corporation, and the classes of stock and the total number of shares. After incorporation, the architects should have a meeting to nominate a board and appoint officers. They should also adopt bylaws which will govern the PC. The bylaws do not have to be filed.

Conflict

As a lawyer representing all the architects, you cannot represent any one of them individually. You owe a fiduciary duty to all of them.

ANSWER TO QUESTION #4 (SAMPLE 2)

1) I would advise the three architects that the best choices for their architectural practice under Georgia law would be a corporation, a professional corporation, or a limited liability company. At issue is which entities provide the most shelter from liability, tax benefits, and ability to exercise control. A corporation could work for the architects. A corporation provides limited liability for its shareholders, officers and directors. If the architects formed a corporation, the corporation could be liable for malpractice claims, but the individual shareholders, officers, and directors would not be, absent intentional wrongful conduct. A professional corporation is, in essence, the same as a corporation but it is created by professionals, meaning lawyers, doctors, engineers, etc. Architects are also professionals, so the P.C. could work for them. The only problem would be how much activity the business manager would have in the corporation. A business manager is not an architect; therefore, he could cause a problem for the architects in creating a P.C. Probably the best entity for the architects to form is a limited liability company. A limited liability company receives the limited liability benefit of a corporation, but also receives pass-through taxation, which is superior to the taxation of a corporation. The "members" of a limited liability corporation do not face personal

liability. As such, the architects would be protected from the malpractice claims of one another, and only the L.L.C. would be liable for debts.

I would advise the architects against creating a common law partnership, limited partnership, or tenancy in common, based on the goals they have elucidated. Again, at issue is the potential liability and lack of control the entities create for the architects. All that is needed for a common law partnership is two or more persons seeking to conduct a business for profit. Thus, the benefit is that they are easy to create because they do not even require a writing, unless for Statute of Fraud purposes. However, under a common law partnership, all partners are general partners. This means that they are jointly and severally liable. If there was a malpractice claim against Tom, the plaintiff could recover from Dick and/or Harry also. Since the architects want to avoid this situation, I would recommend against a common law partnership. Under a limited partnership, there is one or more general partners and one or more limited partners. General partners are jointly and severally liable, while limited partners enjoy limited liability. The problem for the architects would be that the limited partners of the partnership would not be able to exercise any day to day control over the partnership. They receive limited liability because they are expected to remain "silent partners." Tom, Dick, and Harry could not all do their jobs effectively if they were not allowed to exercise day to day control over the partnership. Lastly, I would advise against a tenancy in common. A tenancy in common is when each tenant has a portion of property with no right of survivorship. A tenancy in common is not typically seen as a business entity. The tenants of a tenancy in common are free to alienate their property at will. Therefore, with no discussion or formalities, one of the architects could sell his interest to another. This type of lack of oversight would probably not be desirable based on the architects' goal of wanting to create a "professional practice."

(2) I would recommend that the architects and Sherry create a limited liability partnership. A limited liability partnership is, in essence, a general partnership where all partners get limited liability. This way, Sally could take the reigns as the managing partner of the building, but the architects could have some control if they so chose. Also, they would all be protected, even Sally from the debts and liability claims which arise from ownership of the building.

(a) Sally and their business manager could own stock and be a member of the board of directors or an officer of a corporation. Anyone approved by the corporation can be a shareholder of the corporation, even officers and directors. Also, the incorporators of the corporation (Tom, Dick, and Harry) could name Sally and the business partner as directors of the corporation. Then the board of directors chooses officers.

(b) Sally and their business manager could own stock in the professional corporation but could not be on the Board or be officers. In a professional corporation, the directors and officers must be members of the profession. Since Sally and the business manager are not architects, they could not fill those positions.

(c) Sally and their business manager could own stock and be a member of a limited liability company. As in (3)(a), there are not restrictions on this matter.

(3) If one of the architects were to leave the architectural profession, he could potentially seek a right of appraisal from the Board. Since the architects P.C. is not a public traded corporation, shareholders do not have the option of selling their shares to other architects on the market. He needs to be bought out.

(4) To form a professional corporation, the architects would need to follow the process with which a corporation is created. They would need to file Articles of Incorporation with

the Secretary of State. These Articles would need to include the names of the incorporators, the address of the registered office, the address of the principal place of business, the quantity of stock, etc. They would also need to certify that they are, in fact, professionals with a professional license.

(5) I would need to explain to the architects that I could not effectively represent them individually and the entity at the same time. Under the Georgia Rules of Professional Conduct, lawyers must uphold the profession. As such, lawyers owe a duty to clients to avoid conflicts of interest. If I represent the entity, I must do what is in the best interest of the entity, to the demise of the individual architects. If I were to be given information by one of the architects that was detrimental to the entity, I would have to expose that information to act in the best interests of the entity. I would advise the architects that, should any problems come up in the future, they should each attain separate counsel. Meanwhile, I, as counsel for the entity, will safeguard its interests.

ANSWER TO QUESTION #4 (SAMPLE 3)

1)   Under this scenario, the best choice of business form is probably a limited liability company ("LLC"), followed closely by a professional corporation ("PC"). Based on the professed business and financial objectives of the 3 architects, the business entity will need to provide limited liability to its equity holders, a flexible governance structure conducive to having a "business manager" and the possibility of admitting non-architect equity holders at a future date. The LLC is the only business form mentioned that meets each of these objectives. Under Georgia law, the members of a limited liability company are afforded a liability shield identical to that provided to shareholders in a traditional for-profit corporation. Therefore, in the event of a malpractice claim, the other members of the LLC that are not at fault will have limited liability and will not be financially responsible for the tort beyond the amount of their capital contributions. Of course, a member will always be liable for his own malpractice and no corporate or business form will establish otherwise. The LLC will also provide the architects with an option to be "member-managed" or "manager-managed" which is consistent with their objective of having a professional office manager. Finally, an LLC form will allow other non-architects to become equity investors (provided this is ethical in the profession), which would not be available in a PC, because Georgia law requires that at least 1 director, the President, and all shareholders of a PC be a member of the subject profession. It is also worth noting that an LLC will provide the members with pass-through tax treatment (like a partnership) and requires minimal formality (the members typically only need to file annual reports following the filing of the Articles of Organization).

   As previously stated, a PC would also be an acceptable option, but it would possibly subject the architects to less favorable tax consequences and could also diminish their ability to obtain other equity investors because of the limitation on shareholders (Sally, for example, could not be an equity investor). As to the other discarded forms, a common law partnership (or general partnership) would be a terrible idea because there is no limitation of liability whatsoever, and although a limited partnership would be an incrementally better choice, it too is a terrible idea because it does not afford limited liability to its general partner and any limited partner that exercises control in the business. A corporation might be an option, but for its double taxation and the general formalities involved in comparison to an LLC. A tenancy in common is probably non-sensical if real estate is not involved.

2) I agree with the architects that the building should be held in a separate business entity for both tax and liability purposes. Again, I believe that an LLC provides the best form in this case because it provides limited liability, flexible governance (so that Sally can manage the property), and also allows for other investors that are not architects. The pass through tax benefits of an LLC make it very popular as a real estate holding company in Georgia and elsewhere. Going back to the previous choices presented in Section 1, neither a general partnership or limited partnership is advisable because of liability reasons, a PC is non-sensical because we are talking about the ownership of real property, a for-profit corporation will be subject to double taxation and should rarely be used as a real estate holding company, and a tenancy in common, although growing in popularity, is not a good idea because each of the investors would own a separate divided share with a right to access the whole property. This would be a recipe for controversy.

3(a)   Business Corporation: Yes and Yes. Anyone can be elected a director and anyone can invest, subject to the governing documents of the company and federal and state securities laws.

3(b)   Professional Corporation: No, they could not be shareholders. It is possible that they could be directors because Georgia law requires only that 1 director, the President and all shareholders be members of the profession.

3(c)   Limited Liability Company. No, they could not own stock because an LLC does not issue stock. An LLC issues membership units. However, they both could own membership units, which is the functional equivalent of stock. Similarly, an LLC typically has managers and members, not a board of directors (although you can provide for a board of directors in your Operating Agreement). However, they could serve as managers or on any board that was created.

The company and the existing shareholders would have to buy the stock back, because stock in a professional corporation is not freely transferable like it is with respect to some regular corporations.

Forming a PC is very similar to forming a regular for profit corporation. The incorporators should file Articles of Incorporation with the Georgia Secretary of State pursuant to the Georgia Professional Corporation Act. Like a corporation, I would also recommend that the architects create a set of bylaws that govern the internal affairs of the company, and also put together a Stockholders' Agreement setting forth the relative rights of the various shareholders in relation to one another. They should also issue themselves stock certificates.

As counsel for the company, I would owe a duty to represent the company and to at all times act in the best interests of the company. When you represent the company you do not and cannot represent the individual shareholders because it is an inherent conflict of interest. You may give legal advice to the individuals from time to time, but I would make clear that this advice is being dispensed to them as representatives of the company, and not in any of their individual capacities. I would also have them sign an Engagement Letter to this effect. In the event of a dispute among the 3 individuals in the future, I would explain to them that I cannot and will not represent them and they will have to seek individual counsel, though I can certainly remain as counsel for the company in such dispute.

FEBRUARY 2014 BAR EXAMINATION

QUESTION #1

Mary Murray's husband has died, leaving Mary his entire $4,000,000 estate. Mary, a Georgia resident like her husband, owns $1,000,000 of assets in her own name. She has no descendants, and both of her parents died several years ago. Her only siblings, two brothers, have likewise died. One of her deceased brothers is currently survived by two sons, Able and Bob; and the other brother has one surviving child, a son named Cain.

A cousin from Florida convinced Mary that she needed to set up a revocable trust to hold all of her assets, including those she inherited from her husband. A friend's son just passed the Georgia Bar exam a few months ago and drafted a revocable trust for Mary that is almost identical to the one used by her cousin in Florida. It was the first trust the new attorney had ever prepared. The trust document names Mary as trustee for her lifetime, with her nephew Able as the successor Trustee upon her death. ~ power

Mary inherited the following assets from her husband: a farm worth $2,000,000, a stock portfolio worth $1,000,000, some bank accounts worth $500,000, some Certificates of Deposit worth $400,000, a year-old Lexus worth $50,000, and tangible personal property worth $50,000. The assets that she owns, independent of the inheritance, include the family home, which is solely in her name and worth $500,000, a rental house worth $400,000, $60,000 in a bank account and some furniture, furnishings, jewelry and personal effects worth $40,000. Her husband and she owned nothing together as joint tenants with rights of survivorship.

At the time Mary executed the revocable trust, she signed and recorded a deed transferring the farm she inherited from her husband into the trust and also a deed transferring her interest in her home into the trust. She then wrote out a memo saying that it was her intention to transfer all of the rest of her assets into the trust. She attached this memo to the trust document. Upon the advice of her Florida cousin, she declined to execute a Will, noting to her attorney that she had never actually signed one and did not need one now since she had transferred everything to the trust. The attorney said nothing but simply nodded.

The revocable trust provides that, upon Mary's death, one-half of the trust assets are to be transferred to two charities and the remaining half is to be divided equally among such of her three nephews as survive her. The trust directs that distributions may be made in cash or in-kind, or partially in cash and partially in kind, as the Trustee in the Trustee's sole discretion shall decide. The trust document is silent about what would happen if either charity was not in existence at Mary's death.

It is now a year later, and Mary has just died. Mary died owing no taxes, debts or expenses; and her three nephews survived her. Nothing has changed in the ownership or value of her assets since she executed her revocable trust.

One of the two charitable beneficiaries of her trust, the art museum, was owned by her city.

The city experienced economic reversals beginning in 2008 and has filed for bankruptcy.

The art museum was dissolved six months prior to Mary's death. The other charitable trust beneficiary, Mary's church, argues that it should receive not only its own bequest but also the charitable bequest that would have gone to the museum. A local natural history museum, which is not owned by the city, is contending that, since it is the only other local museum, it should receive the trust's charitable bequest that had been destined for the art museum. The bankruptcy trustee for Mary's city argues it is the successor in interest to the art museum and the bequest should go to pay the city's creditors. The three nephews collectively argue that the bequest should lapse and that they should receive the portion of the trust that would have gone to the art museum.

1.(a) Please discuss which of Mary Murray's assets would be deemed property owned by her revocable trust at her death and why.
(b) If there are no taxes, commissions or other expenses to be paid by the trust, what would be the value of the trust's two charitable bequests and the value of the trust's bequests to each nephew?
(c) How might these bequests be funded, given the nature of the trust assets?
2.(a) Which of Mary's assets, if any, would be part of her probate estate and which part of her intestate estate?
(b) Please explain which individuals or entities would inherit any such non-trust assets and calculate the value of such inherited shares.
3.(a) Which Georgia Court would have jurisdiction to decide the claims over the bequest to the now defunct art museum, and what principles of law might that Court apply in deciding who would be the recipient of the
bequest that had been destined for the art museum?
(b) As succinctly as you can, please describe the strengths and weaknesses of the claims of the four parties which seek to receive the trust bequest that would have gone to the art museum.
4) What ethical issues, if any, might be involved in the attorney's drafting of Mary's revocable trust and his related estate planning advice?

QUESTION #2

On April 17, 2013, there was a flash flood on Charlie's Waterford Farm. All the private access bridges that crossed Waterford Creek and most of the roads accessing them, including Charlie's, were damaged or destroyed by the flood. Charlie's farm was effectively cut off from the outside world. Before Charlie could get his vehicles out of the farm or anyone could come on to the farm, he needed assistance from contractors with heavy equipment and engineering experience to replace or repair his bridge and access road.

Two days after the flood, Charlie received a call from Brian offering to help repair his bridge. Brian and Charlie met at the property to discuss the damage and repairs. That evening, Brian sent an email to Charlie stating, "Will repair your bridge for $20,000." Charlie responded, "$20,000 fee too high for my budget. I can offer you $10,000." Brian responded, "Because of the increased demand for my services due to the flood damages in the area, I'm sorry it is $20,000 or nothing. If you want me to fix your bridge, send me a contract for my approval." After thinking about his options, Charlie emailed Brian, "I accept your terms. A contract follows. Please sign it and send it back as soon as possible."

The next day before the contract from Charlie arrived, Brian accepted an offer from Charlie's neighbor to repair his bridge for $35,000. Brian immediately emailed Charlie, "I cannot sign your contract, I've been offered the job of repairing your neighbor's bridge and I have accepted that offer." Charlie responded, "You can't renege now. We've got a deal for $20,000, and I'm going to hold you to it."

Two days later Charlie contracted with Ronnie, another contractor, to repair the bridge damaged by the flood for a firm price of $30,000. Charlie agreed to pay $5,000 upon execution of the contract and the additional $25,000 upon the completion of the repairs. The bridge repair contract with Ronnie contained the following provision: This contract is the parties' entire agreement. Nothing has been agreed to or is otherwise part of this contract that is not expressly included in it. This contract cannot be amended, varied, modified, or added to in any respect except by a writing signed by both parties.

Seven days after Charlie and Ronnie signed the contract and the work was begun on the repairs to the bridge, there was another flood that did more damage to the bridge and washed out many of Ronnie's repairs completed up to that point.

Ronnie's engineer determined that the second flood resulted in $10,000 more in damage. Ronnie told Charlie that he would proceed with the repairs only if Charlie agreed to pay an additional $5,000, for a total of $35,000. Charlie said he would. When the construction was complete, Charlie refused to pay the $30,000 final payment and tendered only $25,000 explaining he would not honor the verbally-modified agreement.

Charlie contracted with Thurman for $3,000 to repair his access road. This repair included re-contouring the road, cutting in a ditch, and installing a 25-foot galvanized pipe with a 20-inch diameter to carry runoff water under the road. The contract called for Charlie to pay Thurman $1,000 up front and $2,000 upon completion. Upon completion, Charlie discovered Thurman had installed a 20-foot galvanized pipe with a 15-inch diameter instead. The rest of Thurman's work was satisfactory. Charlie refused to pay Thurman the $2,000 final payment because Thurman installed the wrong size pipe.

After all the repairs were completed Charlie comes to your office and solicits your advice regarding the following questions.

1(a) Did Charlie have an enforceable contract with Brian to repair the bridge?
(b) Should he proceed against Brian for the difference in the price with Brian and the contract with Ronnie? Please explain your answers.
2) Is Charlie obligated to pay the additional $5,000 to Ronnie that was agreed upon

after the second flood? Please explain your answer.

3) Is Charlie obligated to pay Thurman the final payment despite the fact that Thurman installed the wrong size pipe? Please explain your answer.

QUESTION #3

Defendant's wife was killed sometime during the evening or early morning hours of January 6 – 7, 2013, by a single gunshot to the back of her head while she was asleep at home in her bed in Macon, Georgia. Defendant called 911 at approximately 1:30 a.m. to report the shooting but was not present when emergency responders arrived. At the scene, a 9mm pistol was discovered under the pillow next to the victim, aimed towards the back of her head. The pillow on which the victim's head had been resting bore bullet entry and exit holes. A single shell casing was found on the floor near the bed, and the gun had a live round in its chamber.

During the trial testimony of the police investigator, the prosecution offered into evidence the bloody pillow on which the victim's head was resting when police arrived at the scene.

A dowel rod was inserted through the pillow, as the police investigator explained, to demonstrate the trajectory of the bullet. Over a timely hearsay objection, the police investigator testified that the crime scene technician's written report stated that the entry and exit holes in the pillow, the straight path of the bullet, the gunpowder markings on the underside of the pillow, and the absence of any other gunshot residue all supported the theory that the shooter had folded a pillow around the back of the victim's head and shot her through the pillow.

The prosecution's firearms expert testified that had the gun discharged from underneath Defendant's pillow, it was unlikely the shell casing would have ejected and a second round cycled into the gun's chamber; rather, the casing would have stuck in the chamber. The prosecution's firearms expert also testified that the gun was in good operating condition and required several pounds of applied force to be fired. Citing *Daubert v. Merrell Dow Pharmaceuticals, Inc.*, the Defense sought to establish on cross-examination that the testimony of the firearms expert was not based upon reliable principles and methods. The trial judge sustained the prosecution's objection to this line of cross-examination, ruling that Daubert does not apply in criminal cases. At trial, the Defendant testified that he was awakened that night by a noise and jumped out of bed, grabbing his gun, which went off as his hands were underneath his pillow. He further testified that he then proceeded to check the rest of the house and came back to discover that the victim had been shot. In rebuttal testimony for the prosecution, the police investigator testified from his incident report that in a statement a few hours after the shooting but before any arrest, the Defendant said that he kept the gun under his pillow for safety and that he was awakened that night by what he thought was a gunshot, jumped out of bed and checked the house but found nothing, and returned to the bedroom where he turned on the light to find his wife shot dead and his gun under the pillow next to her. The trial judge overruled the Defendant's objection that the incident report is inadmissible hearsay. The Defendant made no further objection to the incident report.⁴

Over the objection of defense counsel, the pillow with the dowel rod was sent out with the tangible evidence for the jury's deliberations. ⌐5

The Defendant was found guilty of murder and sentenced accordingly. Less than 30 days have passed since the sentence was entered by the trial judge.

Your senior partner has been contacted by the Defendant's family to undertake the Defendant's representation. He has directed you to prepare a memorandum of law addressing the following:

1) Should the prosecution's rebuttal evidence of the Defendant's pre-custodial statement have been excluded as hearsay? Please explain your answer.
2) Did the trial court err in restricting the Defendant's cross-examination of the prosecution's firearms expert? Please explain your answer.
3) Was the police investigator's testimony regarding his written report hearsay, and should it have been excluded? Please explain your answer.
4) Could trial counsel have objected on any other basis to the police investigator's testimony regarding the contents of his written report? Please explain your answer.
5) Should the Defendant's objection to sending the dowel rod out with the jury have been sustained? Please explain your answer.

QUESTION #4 - Ethics / GA Civ. Pro - $\frac{4.25}{6}$

On October 2, 2010, Arthur was driving southbound in the outside, right-hand lane of I-75 when he was struck suddenly and without warning in the rear by a tractor-trailer rig driven by Bernard. At the time of the collision, Clarence was riding as a passenger in the tractor-trailer rig and was a co-employee of Bernard, both working for Hauling Freight, Inc. As a result of the collision, Arthur's vehicle was knocked across the southbound lanes of I-75 and into a concrete bridge abutment, resulting in a significant brain injury which permanently disabled Arthur.

Many months later, Arthur's son was appointed as his guardian. Due to the extensive nature of Arthur's injuries and the proceedings to have a guardian appointed, Arthur's son did not engage the services of an attorney until two days before the statute of limitations was to expire. Consequently, Arthur's counsel was able to review only the Georgia Motor Vehicle Accident Report before he drafted, signed, and filed a Complaint for Damages against Hauling Freight, Inc. and Bernard. All investigation was done after the filing.

During the course of discovery, the plaintiff's counsel learned that Clarence was terminated by Hauling Freight, Inc. for reasons unrelated to the collision; and Hauling Freight, Inc. did not know where he resided or how he could be located. Plaintiff's counsel hired an investigator who was able to locate Clarence, then residing in Texas.

Clarence was willing to return to Georgia to assist plaintiff's counsel with his investigation. Plaintiff's counsel paid to have Clarence flown to Atlanta, at which time Clarence was taken to the accident site and interviewed by plaintiff's counsel. Thereafter, Clarence gave a recorded statement to plaintiff's counsel. Plaintiff's counsel then notified counsel for Bernard and Hauling Freight, Inc. of Clarence's location, and noticed the deposition of Clarence for a specific date and time.

Defendants' counsel filed a Motion for Protective Order to prohibit the use of any prior statements given by Clarence as a result of the ex parte contact by plaintiff's counsel. A hearing on this motion was scheduled by the Court for 11:00 o'clock a.m. on the day preceding the deposition of Clarence.

Unknown to plaintiff's counsel, defense counsel caused a subpoena to be issued and served on the registrar of the local college that Arthur attended, requiring the registrar to appear at a hearing at 10:00 o'clock a.m. on the same day that the defendants' Motion for Protective Order was to be heard. The subpoena required the registrar to bring a complete copy of Arthur's college transcript to the hearing, or in lieu of his appearance, the registrar was directed to simply forward a copy of that transcript to defense counsel.

No hearing was actually scheduled for 10:00 a.m., nor was any notice of the hearing given to counsel for plaintiff.

1) Discuss the ethical propriety of plaintiff's counsel filing this Complaint for Damages without having conducted any investigation of the facts. After filing this Complaint for Damages, what are his ethical responsibilities as to an investigation and continued litigation?

2) Please discuss the ethical propriety of plaintiff's counsel in contacting Clarence, flying him to Georgia, taking him to the accident scene, interviewing him, and taking a recorded statement from him, prior to notifying defense counsel. How should the judge rule on the Motion for Protective Order?

3) Discuss the ethical propriety of defense counsel's subpoena to the college registrar requiring his attendance and the production of Arthur's transcript at or before a non-existent hearing and without notice to plaintiff's counsel. Further, if the registrar produces the transcript to defense counsel under these circumstances and plaintiff's counsel learns about it after the fact, what is plaintiff's counsel's recourse?

FEBRUARY 2014 BAR EXAMINATION ANSWERS

DISCLAIMER

These are actual answers to essay and MPT items that were written by applicants during this Bar examination. Each of these answers received a high score from the Examiner who wrote and graded the essay question or graded the MPT item. The answers are provided to be helpful to applicants in preparing for a future exam, not to be used to appeal a score received on a prior exam. Pursuant to Part B, Section 13, there are no regrades or appeals after the release of grades. The answers may be printed and circulated.

QUESTION #1 (SAMPLE 1)

1)(a) The $2,000,000 farm and the $500,000 family home would be deemed trust res, or property owned by her revocable trust at her death. These are the only two items that she had physically transferred to the trust at the time of her death.

(b)   If no taxes, commissions, or other expenses are to be paid by the trust, the value of the trusts two charitable bequests would be $750,000 each for a total of $1,250,000 (half of the trust's assets). As Mary was survived by three nephews, the directive of the trust allowed for them each to get an equal share of the other half of the trust assets (1/3 each of $1,250,000).

(c)   To fund these bequests, Mary gave sole discretion to Able as the successor Trustee to make distributions in cash or in kind, or partially in cash and partially in kind, however he sees fit. Given that the trust assets are properties with great value, he may sell the trust assets to get cash to make the distribution equally from there, or if he and the other nephews wanted to keep the house and/or farm, they could likely buy out the other beneficiaries if they so chose and Able decided, in his discretion, that would be feasible.

2(a) All of the remaining assets, with the exception of the farm and Mary's home which were a part of the trust would be pass through intestacy since Mary did not leave a will.

(b)   Under Georgia's Intestacy Statute, since Mary did not have a surviving spouse, children, parents, or siblings, her nephews are the next in line to take. As such, it will no longer be split into half for each of Mary's pre-deceased brothers and then divided to the nephews (per capita/per stirpes), instead, each nephew will take an equal 1/3 share of the remaining total assets (less the farm and house).

3(a) The Georgia Superior court of the county in which the property or defendants lie would be a proper court to have jurisdiction over the claims to the now defunct art museum.

The court would likely apply the doctrine of cy pres to fulfill the trust wishes. The court will apply cy pres in the event of a charitable trust in order to prevent the gift from lapsing if the trust beneficiary no longer exists. The court will normally try to find a replacement charitable trust with a similar trust purpose.

(b) Mary's Church: While a good cause, it is not very similar to the purpose of the gift to the art museum. They are already receiving a significant balance from the trust, but it is a cause Mary supports as noted by her other bequest. Natural History Museum: I believe the Natural History Museum most closely identifies with Mary's original bequest to the art museum. It is the most similar of those vying for the trust assets of the four. It's purpose is likely to preserve historical significance of valuable pieces and works for the future enjoyment and education of the general public--a goal very similar to that of the art museum.

Bankruptcy Trustee: The city owned the art museum, so they could argue that Mary was ultimately gifting the funds to them; however this is not a charitable purpose and a court would not likely find it consistent with Mary's original wishes and purpose.

Three Nephews: The nephews may argue that they are the reasonable beneficiary because they are Mary's closest living kin; however, a court would likely find this would not uphold the charitable trust purpose Mary had in mind. The court will try to come as close as possible to the settlor's original intent.

4. Ethical issues involved in the attorney's drafting of Mary's revocable trust and his related estate planning advice mainly involve his competency. The facts stated that he had just passed the bar and this was the first revocable trust document he had prepared, lending to the fact the was not very experienced in this area, especially in regards to a complicated and valuable trust such as this. Any lawyer is considered competent for the purpose of practicing law; however, he/she must be willing to either decline work until proficient in the area, advise the client at no charge (for his additional studies/learning) he will become competent in the area, or with the client's consent, he will partner with a more knowledgeable attorney in the specific practice area. It seems, given the complexity of this trust, the last option would have been a wise decision. Additionally, the attorney knew she had significant assets and did not advise her to draft a will, he just nodded his head in agreement when she said she no longer needed one since she transferred everything to the trust.

QUESTION #1 (SAMPLE 2)

1(a) The property owned by the trust would be the farm and the home because Mary signed and recorded deeds transferring them into the trust. Although Mary signed a memo of her intent to transfer all of her other assets into the trust, she did not actually transfer any of them. Therefore, all of the other items, the stock portfolio, bank accounts, certificates of deposit, Lexus, personal property and the rental home remain Mary's personal property and are not a part of the trust.

(b) The value of the trust at the time of Mary's death was $ 2,500,000 between the farm and the home. The trust stated that the charities were to split ó of the trust so therefore each charity would receive 1/4 of the total trust. The three surviving nephews were to split of the trust. The nephews would each receive 1/3 of the remaining.

(c) The easiest way for the bequests to be funded would be by selling the property and dividing the proceeds in accordance with the trust. Therefore, each beneficiary would receive cash. The Trustee could also partition the property and deed a portion of the property to each beneficiary of the trust.

2(a) The remaining assets would be a part of Mary's intestate estate because she died without a will. That would include the stock portfolio ($1,000,000), bank accounts from her husband ($500,000), Certificates of Deposit ($400,000), the Lexus ($50,000), personal property from her husband ($50,000), the rental home ($400,000), her bank accounts ($60,000) and her property ($40,000).

(b) Because Mary died intestate, without a will, her estate would be divided among her intestate heirs. Since Mary died without a spouse, children or surviving parents, her estate would go to her siblings equally. Mary had two brothers and therefore, each would be entitled to ó of her estate. Since both brothers predeceased Mary, their share of the estate gets passed to their heirs. Since one brother had 2 sons, Able and Bob would share in their father's of the estate and therefore, they would each receive 1/4 of the entire estate.

Since Cain is the only surviving child of the other brother, he would take the entire. The total amount of the assets in the estate are $2,500,000. Therefore, Cain would take $1,250,000 and Able and Bob would each receive $625,000.

3(a) Since the city where the museums are and the place where Mary died are the same, the Superior Court in the county where that is located would have jurisdiction over the claims. Jurisdiction could also be found in the county where the farm is if that is a different county.

(b) Church- the strength of the claim of the church to receive the trust bequest is that Mary included the church in the original trust and therefore clearly wanted the church to receive money from the trust. The weakness is that if Mary wanted the church to get all the portion delegated to the charities that she would not have included the museum or would have had a provision in the trust that in the event the museum was no longer in existence, that all of the bequest was to go to the church.

Local Natural History Museum –the strength is that the court will look to the intention of the creator of the trust and will try to fulfill that intention when the original intention is no longer viable. In this case, Mary wanted the bequest to go to a local museum and since this is the only other local museum, the bequest should go to it. The weakness is that even though it is the only other local museum, Mary intended for the bequest to go to an art museum and this is a natural history museum so they don't quite have the same purpose.

City-the strength of the argument is that the city owned the museum which the original bequest was left to and therefore should receive that benefit. The weakness is that Mary wanted the bequest to fund an art museum and not to pay off the city's creditors.

Nephews-the strength is that the nephews are Mary's only surviving heirs and the remaining of the trust was left to them. The weakness is that if Mary wanted them to receive a larger portion of the trust she would have established the trust that way.

Also there are anti-lapse statutes in place to ensure Mary's intentions are followed.

4. First, the question states that the attorney had passed the bar but was not clear if he had been sworn in. If not, he is not authorized to practice law in Georgia, which includes drafting the trust and giving estate planning advice. Second, the attorney used a revocable trust that was from Florida. He must be sure that it meets the requirements for Georgia and cannot simply rely on the language and form of the other trust. Since he has not drafted a trust before, he has the obligation of doing his due diligence in researching the criteria.

He can do this by simply researching on his own or consulting with an attorney who has experience in trusts. He should make sure to inform Mary of his novice in this area so that she can obtain other counsel if desired. Third, he should have advised Mary to either transfer all of the assets into the trust or to make a Will. Looking at the trust and memo and saying nothing is still an ethical violation because he should have known that those things were needed in order to protect Mary's wishes and intentions.

QUESTION #1 (SAMPLE 3)

1(a)   The farm and home would likely be the only assets to be included as part of Mary's revocable trust. The creation of a trust requires a settlor, trustee, beneficiary, specific and identifiable trust property (res) and intent to create a trust (shown by specific and enforceable duties for the trustee). In this case, Mary would be the settlor and trustee (the nephew is successor trustee). The charities and nephews would be beneficiaries of the trust. The trust property must be specific and identifiable, and requires a present interest in the property. Here, the facts indicate that Mary properly executed and recorded the deeds transferring her interest in the farm and home to the trust; that is sufficient. Whether the trust contains enforceable duties of the trustee is not clear from the facts. If it does, a trust has been created. If it does not, the trust will fail. The remaining property likely will not be included in the trust because Mary simply executed a memo stating that it was her future intention to transfer the rest of her assets into the trust. A trust requires a present property interest; a promise to transfer a property interest in the future is insufficient.

Accordingly, it is unlikely that this property will constitute the readily identifiable property that a trust requires, and would not be included in the trust.

(b) The value of the trust's two charitable bequests would be half of the trust assets, which is $1.25 million (farm is worth $2 million and home is worth $500,000). The value of the trust's bequests to the beneficiaries would be 1/3 of the $1.25 million, because all three nephews have survived her. Note, however, that Able, as successor trustee, may need to appoint an independent trustee in order for him to reach trust assets as a beneficiary under Georgia law.

(c) The bequests would likely be funded by either granting proportionate property interests in the specific property to each beneficiary as fee simple estates. If issues were to arise with the sharing of the property as co-tenants among the beneficiaries, they could seek to be bought out, for partition in kind, or a complete sale and proportionate distribution of the proceeds.

2(a)   Assuming that the trust was invalid due to failure to state specific property (other than the farm and home), Mary's intestate estate would include her husband's stock portfolio, bank accounts, Certificates of Deposit, year-old Lexus, and tangible personal property (worth $2 million total). Her intestate estate would also include the rental home, bank account, and the furniture, furnishings, jewelry and personal effects (worth $500,000 total). None of Mary's assets would pass through her probate estate because she did not create a valid will. A will requires a writing, signed by the testator, witnessed by 2 witnesses, and signed by 2 witnesses. Mary created no such writing, and as a result, all of her property not in the trust ($2.5 million) would pass intestate.

(b)   The individuals that would inherit Mary's probate estate are her nephews, Able, Bob and Cain. If the decedent dies without any surviving lineal descendants or surviving parents, the decedent's siblings will take from the decedent's estate per capita, and the siblings' children will take per stirpes. But in Georgia, if the decedent's siblings have all predeceased, the decedent's nieces and nephews will take equal shares of the decedent's estate. In this case, Mary died with no surviving lineal descendants or parents, and her siblings have both pre-deceased her. As a result, Mary's three nephews will take equal shares (each 1/3) of Mary's $2.5 million intestate estate.

3(a)   The Superior Court would have jurisdiction to decide the claims over the bequest to the now defunct Georgia art museum, because the Georgia Superior Court has exclusive jurisdiction over cases involving title to land. Here, the art museum would be claiming title to the trust property, which is the farm and home. As a result, the suit involves title to land and belongs in the superior court.

   In deciding who would be the recipient of the bequest to the art museum, the court will apply the cy pres doctrine. The cy pres doctrine applies where the trust beneficiary no longer exists. The court will look to the settlor's intent and substitute another charitable beneficiary that is most closely aligned with the settlor's original intent.

(b)   The church may argue that because it is already a trust beneficiary, it was Mary's intent for the trust to benefit the church. On the other hand, Mary's specifically chose to include the art museum, which arguably serves a different purpose than the church. Accordingly, using cy pres to benefit the church may not be in line with Mary's intent. Local history museum has a strong argument that it was Mary's intent to benefit the arts and museums, and it is the appropriate cy pres beneficiary. But it is not owned by the city, and Mary may have intended to benefit the city. The bankruptcy trustee could argue that Mary intended to benefit the city, and that providing to the city's creditors is most in line with her intent. This seems unlikely to prevail because the cy pres doctrine is used for a substitute charitable purpose. The nephews can argue that they should take as they were named beneficiaries under the trust. But cy pres is meant to substitute another charity.

4)   A lawyer must be competent in his representation of a client. Competency

requires the requisite knowledge, skill, and time for the representation. A lawyer may become competent, if he is not already, by gaining the knowledge and skill through study (with no cost to the client) or by associating with an attorney that is competent (with the client's consent). Here, the friend's son may not be competent to have prepared a trust. He just passed the bar exam and has only drafted one other trust. In addition, the trust he drafted appears to be identical to the first trust, thus indicating that he did not tailor the trust to his client's needs.

In addition, the lawyer could be liable because his conduct implied to Mary that she did not need a will. Had the attorney been competent, he would have known that the trust was invalid as to much of Mary's property and a will was required. A lawyer has a duty to zealously represent his client, and the simple nodding back to Mary in response to her statement may not satisfy this high standard.

QUESTION #2 (SAMPLE 1)

1(a)   The issue is whether Charlie had an enforceable contract with Brian to repair the bridge. An enforceable contract requires mutual assent in the form of an offer, acceptance of that offer, and sufficient consideration. Brian's initial email offering to repair Charlie's bridge for $20,000 was an offer, which Charlie rejected in his response when he said $20,000 was too high. Charlie then counter-offered Brian $10,000, which Brian then rejected. The rejection was unequivocal, as Brian refused to take less than $20,000.

Brian's statement, "if you want me to fix your bridge, send me a contract for my approval," should probably not be construed as another counteroffer because it did not create a power of acceptance in Charlie. He merely invited Charlie to send him further offers if he wanted Brian to fix his bridge. Because there was no outstanding offer, Charlie's email "accepting his terms" did not operate as an acceptance, and there was no enforceable contract. It should be noted that if there was an offer, Charlie's email would have created a contract under the mailbox rule, even though Brian accepted an offer from Charlie's neighbor before the contract from Charlie arrived.

(b) Because Charlie did not have an enforceable contract with Brian, he should not proceed against him for the difference in price with Brian and the contract with Ronnie.

However, assuming that Charlie and Brian did have an enforceable contract for repair of the bridge, Charlie would be able to point to the contract with Ronnie in calculating his expectation damages for breach of contract (because Brian did not perform by undertaking the repairs for Charlie). Expectation damages seek to put a party in the place he would be had the contract been performed. If Ronnie ultimately fixed the bridge for $30,000, Charlie would be entitled to the $10,000 difference in the two contract prices.

2)   The issue is whether Charlie must pay Ronnie the additional $5000, which the parties verbally agreed on following the second flood. As an initial matter, the parol

evidence rule bars evidence of prior written or prior or contemporaneous oral statements to modify the terms of a fully integrated agreement. The bridge repair contract with Ronnie contains a merger clause stating that the contract constitutes the parties' entire agreement, and that the contract could not be modified except by a writing signed by both parties. The parol evidence does not bar evidence of Charlie and Ronnie's oral modification because it happened after the execution of the initial written contract. Because this is a service contract that can be completed within a year, the original contract does not fall within the statute of frauds. The merger clause notwithstanding, no writing is needed to evidence the modification.

Accordingly, whether Charlie must pay the extra $5000 depends on whether there was sufficient consideration for the modification as required under common law.

Adequate consideration, a necessary component of an enforceable contract, consists of either a legal benefit to the promisor or a legal detriment to the promisee. Under the pre existing duty rule, agreeing to undertake a task that one was already legally obligated to do (by prior contract or otherwise) is insufficient consideration. However, courts have not strictly enforced this rule by construing the new agreement as involving a different or additional performance than that initially agreed upon. Here, the parties had not contemplated the second flood which resulted in $10,000 in extra damage to the bridge and washed out Ronnie's repairs. Agreeing to the additional performance required by the second flood may be considered sufficient to constitute adequate consideration to support the modification.

Nevertheless, even if the oral modification is found to be unenforceable, Ronnie may be able to recover the reasonable value of the benefits that he conferred on Charlie by doing the additional repairs under a restitutionary theory.

3) The issue is whether Charlie must pay Thurman the final payment despite the fact that Thurman installed the wrong size pipe. In contracts not for the sale of goods, including construction contracts, a party is only excused from performing due to the other party's breach if that breach was material. If the breach was not material and the breaching party substantially performed his contractual obligations, the innocent party may not withhold performance (in this case, payment for services) but may still sue for the damages caused by the breach. Here, whether Charlie must perform under the contract depends on whether Thurman's breach was material. In repairing Charlie's access road, Thurman re- contoured the road, cut in a ditch, and installed a pipe to carry runoff water under the road. Thurman's repair work was satisfactory except for his installation of a 20-foot pipe with a 15-inch diameter instead of a 25-foot pipe with a 20-inch diameter. The facts do not state that the precise length and diameter of the pipe was crucial to its purpose, or otherwise that the actually installed pipe did not carry the runoff water under the road. Under these facts, a court is likely to find that Thurman's breach was not material and that Charlie was not justified in withholding the $2000 final payment as a result. This is particularly true because the costs of tearing out the pipe and redoing the whole job is probably unreasonably high in comparison to any decrease in value of the property from the wrong pipe.

QUESTION #2 (SAMPLE 2)

1(a)   No, Charlie did not have an enforceable contract with Brian to repair the bridge. Under Georgia law, parties to a contract enter into an agreement, by mutual assent, supported by consideration before contract exists. The primary issue in Charlie's negotiations with Brian is the evidence supports a finding that there was a lack of mutual assent between Brian and Charlie.

At the end of the negotiations and after the first offer from Brian, which was rejected expressly and by implication through Charlie's counteroffer, Brian once again made a counteroffer to Charlie by writing "I am sorry it is $20k or nothing. If you want me to fix your bridge, send me a contract for my approval." Although Brian referenced a price from earlier in negotiations, this counteroffer from Brian was not unconditional. Brian solicited an offer/counteroffer from Charlie and placed a condition on any possible agreement that Charlie needed to send Brian a contract for Brian's approval. Although Charlie wrote back "I accept your terms. A contract follows" Charlie did not actually accept any valid offer to enter into a contract. He merely acknowledged that he understood what was necessary (condition precedent) for him to make an offer/counteroffer to Brian. Charlie actually made a counteroffer to Brian by sending Brian a contract for Brian's approval. Brian accepted the offer from Charlie's neighbor before he even received the new offer from Brian.

(b) Although the decision is Charlie's, I would not recommend that he proceed in an action against Brian for the difference in the price he would have paid Brian and the price he agreed to pay Ronnie. As stated in the answer above, a court is unlikely to find an enforceable written agreement between the parties due to a lack of agreement and lack of mutual assent.

Charlie also has little support for an action in quasi contract, little support for any tort claim and little support for an action for any type of equitable recovery. There is little evidence to support a finding that Charlie reasonably relied, in any meaningful way on any representation or statement by Brian.

2)   Yes. Charlie will likely be required to pay up to $5000 as damages to Ronnie. Although Ronnie bore the risk of loss at the time of the second flood, because under Georgia law contractors retain the risk of loss during construction projects, this will likely be negated by a finding that Ronnie and Charlie either entered into an agreement to modify the original contract price because he arguably waived the contractual provision requiring amendments be in writing or, under quasi-contract or equitable theories, because Ronnie relied to his detriment on Charlie's promise to pay the increased price.

Ronnie could argue that, after the second flood, he offered to amend the contract price in his agreement with Charlie and Charlie expressly accepted his offer to modify the contract. Charlie said he would pay the increased price. A court could find that this constituted an agreement whereby Ronnie made an offer and Charlie accepted the offer and could find consideration in the continued construction of the bridge and the increased price. Ronnie could effectively argue that Charlie waived the provision of the contract requiring amendments to be in writing by agreeing to the new price and knowingly allowing Ronnie to complete the project under the proposed new terms.

Ronnie could also attempt to recover under quasi-contract theories and estoppel theories.

Ronnie should argue that there was an agreement to modify the price term of the contract between the parties, he reasonably relied on that agreement and Charlie's representation that Charlie would pay the new price, and, as a result of his reliance, he suffered a detriment. Although Ronnie might not be able to recover the full $5,000 simply because the parties agreed to a $5000 increase in price, Ronnie might be able to recover the value of his improvements to Charlie's property and the value of his work.

3) Charlie is likely obligated to pay Thurman some, if not all, of the final payment despite the pipe size error. Under the facts presented, Thurman substantially performed on his contract with Charlie. A party substantially performs when it adequately performs all of the material terms of a contract, even if there is a slight variation in materials used. If a court finds that the pipe size was a material term of the contract, Thurman might be liable for value of the repair to the access road with the 20-inch pipe less the value of the repair with the 15-inch pipe. Thurman could also just repair and replace with the right pipe within a reasonable time to cure his performance defect. If the contract terms prevent Thurman from recovering, he might seek equitable recovery against Charlie for the value of his work on Charlie's property.

QUESTION #2 (SAMPLE 3)

1. (a) Probably not. Charlie and Brian likely did not have an enforceable contract. A contract requires and offer and acceptance. An offer is an unequivocal manifestation of an intent to enter into a deal, and the offeror dictates the terms of acceptance. However, the contract is not formed until the offeree has actually accepted. Here, Charlie initially invited an offer from Brian, and Brian offered to fix the bridge for $20K. Charlie rejected the offer, however, and instead counter- offered $10K. The rejection of the offer and extension of the $10K counter-offer effectively put the ball in Brian's court, and Brian rejected that offer. The issue is whether Brian's response thereafter that only $20K would be acceptable was actually an offer, or whether he had extended an invitation to Charlie to offer him $20K. If the email was an "offer," then under the mailbox rule, Charlie's sending the contract would have constituted acceptance as of the moment he put the contract in the mail under the mailbox rule.

Under the circumstances, however, the email response was likely an invitation for an offer, because it stated that Charlie would need to "contract for approval" before they could move forward. This suggests that he was not quite ready to deal, but rather wanted to see a contract and approve it first. Therefore, they did not have an enforceable contract.

(b) Because of my conclusion that they did not have a contract, Brian should likely not proceed against Charlie for the difference in price between the contract with Ronnie and the contract with Brian. Nevertheless, I acknowledge that there is merit to both arguments (whether they had a contract), and, therefore, pursuing such an action would not be frivolous.

2) The issue here is whether Charlie and Ronnie's verbal agreement constitutes an enforceable promise. If it was an effective modification of the contract, then it will be enforceable. If not, Ronnie may still be able to recover on a theory of quasi contract or promissory estoppel.

Here, the merger clause provides that the entire agreement is in the written contract and requires that it cannot be amended except by writing signed by both parties. This clause is enforceable and a Georgia court is likely to uphold it.

Because the oral modification did not comport with the terms of the merger clause, the contract does not require that Charlie pay the additional $5,000. Nevertheless, Ronnie can likely still recover it based on a theory of promissory estoppel or quasi-contract. Under promissory estoppel, a party's otherwise unenforceable promise may be enforced if the other party reasonably and foreseeably relied on the promise, and if allowing the promise to go unfulfilled would result in unjust enrichment. Similarly, quasi-contract allows for enforcement where a person has rendered performance or partial performance based on a non-enforceable promise, but one on which the person reasonably and foreseeable relied. It also requires a finding of unjust enrichment.

Here, promissory estoppel may apply because Charlie promised to pay the extra $5,000. Ronnie relied on that promise. His reliance on that promise was foreseeable for several reasons. First, as they were already in a contract, Charlie had a duty of good faith to Ronnie with respect to contract matters. Additionally, because Ronnie and Charlie had been dealing in the past, Ronnie could reasonably and foreseeably have relied on that record of past dealing (i.e. the initial contract phase). Finally, it was foreseeable to Charlie that Ronnie would rely on the promise because Charlie clearly intended for Ronnie to finish the work on the bridges, and the promise of extra money was negotiated after an unforeseen event to effectuate finishing the repairs. Unjust enrichment will be the crucial factor here. Given the additional damage, unjust enrichment should be easy to meet. Essentially, Ronnie is having to repair an additional $10,000 of damage caused by an outside circumstance after he had already begun a repair, and he only demanded an extra $5K for the work. Under these circumstances, promissory estoppel would likely allow Ronnie to pay even in the absence of an actually enforceable contract.

Similarly, quasi-contract may apply here because Ronnie had already performed by repairing the additional damage in reasonable and foreseeable reliance on Charlie's promise of additional money. Unjust enrichment would likely result if Charlie did not have to pay the additional $5,000, as explained above.

3) Whether Charlie is obligated to pay Thurman will depend on the nature of Thurman's breach. That is, whether it was material. The contract here specified the size pipe to be used, and Thurman installed one that was smaller. This undoubtedly was a breach, as the installed pipe does not conform with the contract terms. However, it will likely be material only if the smaller pipe affects the value or performance of the repaired road. As Thurman completed construction, he is likely

entitled to payment of some amount. But if the smaller pipe resulted in damages, Charlie can probably reduce the amount of payment by the damages. If this results in the pipe being totally nonfunctional or not up to a code or ordinance, he can likely require that Thurman replacement the entire thing with the correct size pipe for the original contract price of $3K. In any event, Charlie will have to prove that the breach is material and then may be able to withhold payment if it was.

QUESTION #3 (SAMPLE 1)

TO: Senior Partner
FROM: Examinee
DATE: February 25, 2014
RE: Murder Appeal

This memo will address the issues that Senior Partner has asked me about. Should the prosecution's rebuttal evidence of the Defendant's pre-custodial statement have been excluded as hearsay?

(1) Yes. Hearsay is an out-of-court statement, made by the declarant, to prove the truth of the matter asserted. Hearsay is not admissible unless an exception applies. Exceptions include admissions, statements with legal effect, and testimonial prior consistent or inconsistent statements (prior consistent statements may be introduced to rehabilitate a witness, and prior inconsistent statements need to have been given under oath in a proceeding in which the opposing party had ample opportunity to cross-examine the declarant). Furthermore, a statement will be allowed if it is otherwise hearsay but it is not being introduced for a hearsay use: In other words, if the statement is not being introduced to prove the truth of the matter, it may be admitted as long as its admission does not violate other court rules, such as lack of relevance.

The statement does not appear to fall under a hearsay exception. Moreover, the statement arises from a police report, and police reports themselves may not be admitted in a criminal case.

The prosecution's rebuttal evidence of the Defendant's pre-custodial statement should have been excluded as hearsay.

Did the trial court err in restricting the Defendant's cross examination of the prosecution's firearms expert?

(2) Yes. The purpose of cross examination is to question the testimony that the opposing party introduced through direct examination of its witness. Here, the prosecution was allowed to show, through expert testimony (therefore testimony that would likely be given great weight by the jury, as the testimony is from a witness that the Court has accepted as an expert), the angle of the gun fired and that the gun would have required several pounds of force to be fired. Obviously, this testimony, if

true, seriously increases the chance that the Defendant is guilty of murder. Therefore, cross examination of this expert was very important to the Defendant's case, and the Court nevertheless restricted the Defendant's cross examination, even though such cross examination was surely well within the scope of what the State introduced through its expert witness.

Moreover, the Court restricted the Defendant's cross examination on a Daubert ground, stating that Daubert does not apply to criminal cases. Here, the relevant legal principle from Daubert is of the scientific and technical reliability of tests, and, presumably the State's expert witness relied on such tests in the testimony.

Moreover, the relevant Daubert test is not subject to restriction under whether its principles arise in a criminal or in a civil case: It is allowed in criminal and civil cases.

The Court erred in restricting the Defendant's cross examination of the prosecution's firearms expert.

(3) Was the police investigator's testimony regarding his written report hearsay, and should it have been excluded?

As discussed above, police reports are inadmissible hearsay, as police reports do not fall within an exception to the hearsay rule. However, if the police officer could not presently recall the events in question, he could have been shown the police report to refresh his memory, but that report could not have been introduced into evidence (absent a showing that the police officer still could not recall what the report was supposed to refresh his memory of, but only then on the Past Recollection Recorded Exception, upon a showing that the report had been "adopted" by the officer, and that it did indeed show what the officer could no longer recall).

However, as to the technician's written report, the expert testimony is allowed, and that report, while itself not admissible, might show similar things that the testimony would show.

Of course, the expert testimony would have to arise from tests or methods that other experts in the field use.

Could trial counsel have objected on any other basis to the police investigator's testimony regarding the contents of his written report?

(4) Yes. Trial counsel should have objected on the ground that the expert's testimony was unfairly prejudiced to the defendant, and that prejudice outweighed the probative value of the expert testimony. The evidence was prejudicial because it clearly suggested that the gun had been intentionally fired at the Defendant's wife, and that gun was the gun under the Defendant's bed. The Defendant showed that he had been asleep when the gun went off, and the State's witness' testimony nevertheless went to the gun's intentional firing without even so much as laying a proper foundation for introducing testimony that the gun was taken out from under the Defendant's pillow and intentionally fired in the first place.

Should the Defendant's objection to sending the dowel rod out with the jury have been sustained?

(5) No. The dowel rod was demonstrative evidence, and, as such, was to be introduced only for the State's explanation of how the bullet entered the victim's head. The dowel rod was inserted through the pillow during the police officer's testimony to

supplement the police officer's testimony and to provide a visual. The dowel rod actually has nothing to do with the evidence that was found at the crime scene. Accordingly, the Court should not have permitted the dowel rod to go out to the jury.

QUESTION #3 (SAMPLE 2)

To: Senior Partner
From: Applicant
Re: Defendant's Trial

You have asked me to prepare a memorandum of law addressing certain evidentiary objections during our Defendant's trial.

i) Prosecution Rebuttal Evidence
The first issue is whether the prosecution's rebuttal evidence should have been excluded as hearsay. It was hearsay and it should have been excluded. Under the Rules of Evidence in Georgia, hearsay is an out-of-court statement offered in court to prove the matter asserted. The defendant's statement about his activities that night would get to be admissible as statements of a party, or admissions. Even if they fall into the definition of hearsay, they will always be admissible and are not regarded as hearsay evidence. The testimony may also be considered impeachment evidence because its prior inconsistent evidence by the Defendant. Defendant claims at trial that he heard a noise and grabbed his gun to investigate and returned to a dead wife. The investigator's report, however, shows that the defendant initially testified that he did not take the gun with him when he investigated the house. In Georgia, hearsay evidence may come in as impeachment and substantive evidence if the evidence is of a prior inconsistent statement. The inconsistent statement here does seem material-- how the murder weapon discharged and how and by whom it was used. However, in order to get evidence in this way, the testifying witness must have an opportunity to deny or explain his answer. The facts do not indicate that this happened in the trial, thus, the police incident report is hearsay, and should have been excluded.

ii) Daubert In Criminal Cases
The trial court did err in denying cross-examination. The trial judge is correct in that the Daubert case and its protocols for an evidentiary hearing to establish the bonafides of an expert's testimony is inapplicable to criminal trials in Georgia.

However, in Georgia, cross-examination is wide open and not limited to the direct examination (like other jurisdictions and the Federal Rules). The defense sought to impeach the expert's testimony. In Georgia, an expert may give his opinion if the subject matter of that opinion relates to some specialized knowledge involving some technical skill or scientific trade and that opinion will help the trier of fact come to a resolution in matters of fact. Here, the prosecutor's expert was allowed to testify to his knowledge of firearms and how they operate or do not operate.

If the expert was qualified, then the defense attorney already had his opportunity to attack the experts experience and qualifications. That, however, does not preclude the defense attorney from poking holes in an expert's conclusions and methods. As a result, the trial court likely erred in stopping the cross-examination. The better practice would have been to sustain the objection as to the applicability of Daubert.

(iii) Investigator's Written Report

The Investigator's report is hearsay. It should have been excluded. Hearsay evidence may still be admissible if it falls into certain exceptions. It seeks to bring in out of court statements to prove the matters in which they assert--namely that the Defendant. These statements are coming from a police investigator's incident report. The contents of the police investigator's incident report are hearsay-- because they are being offered to prove what the investigator put down was actually what happened. However, the contents may fall into a hearsay exception. The incident report might be a business record kept by the police in their daily course of business. However, the prosecution would have had to lay the foundation for a business record. In fact, police investigative reports cannot fall under this exception in criminal cases. In addition, since the investigator was testifying, the incident report might have been refreshing recollection--which allows any document to be used to assist a testifying witness remember something that they once remembered but now forgot. Again, this requires foundation where the prosecution would have had to show that the investigators forgot his testimony. The document used in his case may be anything that can refresh. The contents of the incident report might also come as past recollection recorded evidence--which as a hearsay exception, applies when the testifying witness cannot remember what they wrote in the past when it was fresh in their mind and they knew to be true. Even with the document at hand, the testifying witness cannot remember so the evidence is read into the record. This is also inapplicable. However, a witness cannot simply testify from a document on the stand. Outside of these ways to get in the evidence, the contents would be deemed hearsay and the testimony based on them inadmissible.

(iv) Objections to Police Investigator's Testimony

One objection is that a witness cannot testify directly from a written document on the stand. Also, defense counsel might be able to raise a Confrontation Clause issue with the report.

The Confrontation Clause protects criminal defendants from testimonial evidence presented against them if they do not have the opportunity to confront such evidence. Here it seemed that defendant did have an opportunity to cross-examine the witness on the contents of the report. Trial counsel could have also objected to the incident report as a prior inconsistent statement because there is nothing in the evidence to indicate that defendant was given the opportunity to either explain or deny that he made a different statement then the one he made at trial. At trial, of course, defendant had grabbed his gun and went to investigate, raising the inference that someone else shot his wife.

(v) Dowel Rod

The objection to sending the dowel rod should have been sustained. The dowel rod was not physical evidence gathered from the defendant's house and properly authenticated.

The pillow itself was physical evidence and if the prosecution could show that it was the pillow from the night of the shooting then it could come in. However, the dowel rod was demonstrative evidence showing the trajectory of the bullet prepared by the police investigator. Demonstrative evidence may be used, if the foundation is laid that its similar and like the conditions present at circumstances at issue--here at the night of the murder.

However, demonstrative evidence may not go in with the jury.

QUESTION #3 (SAMPLE 3)

1) No, the defendant's pre-custodial statement should not have been excluded as hearsay because it was otherwise admissible. Specifically, hearsay is an out of court statement admitted for the truth of the matter asserted. Here, the defendant's pre-custodial statement was hearsay because it was an out of court statement and was being admitted for the truth of the matter asserted, but it should not have been excluded on the basis that it was hearsay because it qualified as an admission by a party opponent. Admissions by a party opponent are statements that are made by a party to the case, in which case such statements are admissible. They need not be against interest in order to be admissible. In fact, admissions by a party opponent are always admissible. Additionally, it should be noted that since it was a pre-custodial statement there will not be any issues with Miranda.

Furthermore, if hearsay is being offered for some non-hearsay purpose then it may be admissible. For instance, since the pre-custodial statement was being introduced on rebuttal, it is likely that the prosecution was trying to use the statement to impeach the defendant's trial testimony since the statement differed from the testimony at trial. This would be a proper use of hearsay at trial because prior inconsistent statements are admissible. However, one usually has to confront the witness about the statement and give them an opportunity to explain, which doesn't appear to have happened in this case. Nevertheless, although hearsay, it should not have been excluded because it was an admission by a party opponent.

2) No, Daubert does not apply in criminal trials in GA, only in civil trials. However, the criminal court does require that there be some level of scientific reliability to be admissible. Dauber does apply to criminal trial under the Federal evidence rules, which require that an expert's opinions be based on reliable principles and methods, which typically means those generally accepted by the scientific community. While GA has adopted a majority of the Federal evidence rules as of 2013, it has not adopted the use of Daubert in criminal trials.

Therefore, the trial court did not err in limiting the cross-examination of the firearms expert on the basis that Daubert is inapplicable in criminal trials.

3) Assuming this question is referring to the police investigator's testimony as to his

incident report and not his testimony regarding the report of the crime scene technician in paragraph two, the incident report was hearsay. Hearsay is when an out of court statement is being offered for the truth of the matter asserted. Here, the incident report was being offered for it's truth. However, it is possible that the officer's testimony can come in if it qualifies under some other exception or non-hearsay use. For instance, the statement in the report by the defendant could qualify as an admission by a party opponent which is an exception to the hearsay rule and thus the officer's testimony as to this statement would be admissible. Additionally, it appears that the officer's testimony, at least with regard to the defendant's statement, could have qualified for admission as a prior inconsistent statement because it was different from what the defendant testified to at trial. In GA, prior inconsistent statements are admissible for both their substantive and impeachment use.

Thus, this statement may have been introduced by the prosecution as a prior inconsistent statement on rebuttal to impeach the defendant's trial testimony. However, you usually have to give the party being impeached the opportunity to admit, deny, or explain the prior inconsistent statement which it does not appear was done in this case. However, it still appears that the officer's testimony would have qualified as an admissible admission by a party opponent. Further, the incident report may have qualified under the public records exception and thus would have been admissible even though hearsay. Finally, it is possible that the court could have applied the past recollection recorded exception. This exception requires that the declaring have personal knowledge, that the writing was made at a time when the information was fresh in the witness's mind, and that the declaring acknowledge that this is in fact the writing that was made. Here, all of those requirements are met.

4) Trial counsel could have also objected to the officer's testimony regarding the contents of the officer's incident report on the basis that such testimony violates the best evidence rule. This rule requires that before a witness may testify to the contents of a writing, the writing itself, or a copy, must be produced. Here, the officer was allowed to testify to the contents of the writing without first having to produce the writing which violates the best evidence rule. Or on the basis that the defendant was not given an opportunity to admit, deny, or explain the inconsistent statement.

5) Yes, I believe that the defense's objection to sending the dowel rod and pillow out with the jury should have been sustained. Generally, only actual evidence from the crime may be provided to the jury during deliberations. The dowel rod, in this case, was not part of the actual evidence from the crime and instead was used as part of an investigative technique by the crime scene technician to determine the trajectory of the bullet. This should not have been sent back with the jury because it was not actual evidence from the crime.

Additionally, the presence of the dowel rod poses the additional problem that jurors may be tempted to try and conduct their own "trajectory investigations" during deliberations now that they the dowel rod and the pillow in the jury room. This would certainly taint the jury verdict if such action were to occur.

QUESTION #4 (SAMPLE 1)  810 words

1) Ethical propriety of filing the complaint without investigating & responsibilities as to an investigation and continued litigation.

An attorney has a duty to the court to ensure that he files meritorious claims, and abstains from engaging in any fraud on the court or on opposing parties. An attorney also has an obligation to act competently, which requires an attorney to determine that his client's lawsuits are not frivolous or intended to unduly harass an opposing party. In all aspects, an attorney must act reasonably while still protecting the rights of his client. Here, P's counsel did not engage in a complete investigation of the facts underlying the personal injury lawsuit prior to filing the lawsuit. This is because counsel only had two days in which to prepare and file the complaint, in order to satisfy the applicable statute of limitations. As running afoul of a statute of limitations can have dire consequences for a client, it was imperative that P's counsel file the complaint immediately. P's counsel did not file the complaint completely without basis. Rather, he reviewed the Georgia Motor Vehicle Accident Report, which presumably gave a general overview of the accident and attendant damages. Thus, as P's counsel engaged in as much due diligence as was possible within the 2 days prior to the running of the statute of limitations, he acted reasonably and ethically when filing the complaint.

P's counsel's obligations did not end there; however. Rather, P's counsel was subsequently obligated to engage in a meaningful investigation of the facts underlying the complaint, to make sure that the lawsuit was filed without an improper purpose. Here, P's counsel investigated the merits of the claim after filing the complaint, and made the decision not to dismiss. As an investigation appears to have been promptly done after the complaint was filed, P's counsel acted ethically. In the event that the investigation uncovered facts that contradicted the complaint or established that the lawsuit was not meritorious, P's counsel would have been obligated to disclose such information, amend the complaint, and even dismiss if necessary (or withdraw).

2) Ethical propriety of contacting, flying, and interviewing Clarence without notifying D & ruling on Protective Order.

Attorneys are not ethically allowed to contact parties that are represented by counsel. This normally includes employees of an opposing party. However, this prohibition does not extend to individuals who are not represented by counsel, and are not employees of an opposing party.

Here, P's counsel contacted Clarence in order to interview him concerning the accident that is the subject of ongoing litigation. Clarence is not represented by counsel, so P's counsel is not prohibited from contacting him on account of representation. Similarly, Clarence is not an employee of Hauling Freight, though he was an employee at the date the accident occurred. It appears clear that Hauling Freight does not consider Clarence to be its employee currently, nor does it contend that it represents Clarence. If it did, then Hauling Freight certainly would have known where Clarence lived, and would have been in contact with him concerning this lawsuit. There is accordingly no prohibition preventing P's counsel from directly contacting Clarence to obtain a witness interview. In addition, there is no prohibition that prevents P's counsel from paying for Clarence's transportation and likely lodging in GA while the witness interview occurs. P's counsel was not paying Clarence for testimony, rather, he was covering reasonable expenses. There is also nothing improper about visiting the scene of the accident, or about taking a recorded statement. Furthermore, there is nothing improper about noticing Clarence's deposition.

P's counsel was simply developing P's case and preparing for the deposition when taking the witness interview, as is required of an attorney.

Accordingly, as P's counsel did not violate any ethical obligations (though it may have been more courteous of counsel to contact opposing counsel first), the Court should deny the Motion for Protective Order. Regardless, P's counsel will likely be able to elicit the same testimony from Clarence at deposition and not run afoul of any protective order. Further, even in the absence of a protective order, Hauling Freight's counsel will still be able to object to the previous declaration during the witness interview on substantive grounds at trial.

3) Ethical propriety of D's subpoena to college, non-existence hearing, without notice to P & P's recourse. A subpoena may be issued in order to obtain documents from a third party (note: in GA, a request for production is sufficient to obtain such documents, unlike in federal court where a subpoena is required). The subpoena must be served on the opposing side. This is practically because the opposing side may have grounds to move for a protective order, or to quash the subpoena prior to the production date. Thus, it was unethical for D's counsel to subpoena college registrar documents without serving that subpoena on P's counsel.

It was furthermore unethical for D's counsel to advise the college that a hearing would occur if the college failed to produce the transcript, when there was no such hearing set or even contemplated. That is an attempt to strong arm the college into producing documents in order to avoid a costly and time consuming personal appearance, and is inappropriate. D's counsel did not intend to have a hearing, and that is evident from the fact that D's counsel already had another hearing at the same time and date of the hearing set forth on the subpoena. D's counsel acted improperly when sending the subpoena.

There are a couple of avenues that P can pursue in order to obtain recourse. First, if P's counsel discovers the subpoena, he may be able to prevent production by filing a Motion for Protective Order or Motion to Quash. The deadline by which to respond to the subpoena should be extended and should run from the date P's counsel obtained notice of the subpoena. P's counsel should also request that D and D's counsel be sanctioned for their malfeasence. Second, if the transcript is actually produced, P's counsel should move to exclude the transcripts as they were improperly obtained. P should also request sanctions as set forth above.

QUESTION #4 (SAMPLE 2) 430 words

1) Typically counsel should investigate claims before filing them to determine whether the claim is valid or frivolous. But in this case it was reasonable for the attorney to file without investigating in order to file by the statute of limitations deadline. Even with the limited time period, counsel was able to review the accident report and make some limited determination concerning the validity of the claim. Like any attorney, counsel has a continuing duty to investigate and determine the claims are valid or withdraw the complaint.

Thus, counsel must continue to investigate the claims, conduct a thorough investigation of the validity of the claims, and take steps to withdraw from representation or convince the client the claim is invalid and withdraw the complaint. Continuing to pursue the claim would be unethical and could subject the attorney to sanctions.

2) Counsel's interview of Clarence without Defendant's knowledge was ethically acceptable. Clarence did not represent the defendant at that time, was not employed there, and did not have any further connection with the Defendant. Clarence was not a representative or agent of the Defendant and Defendant's counsel did not represent him. Nor was there any indication that Clarence was represented by counsel. Employees may be represented by counsel if they were involved in the accident. Here, however, Clarence was not directly involved, just a passenger, and without further involvement he is simply a witness to the event. Both Defendant and Plaintiff may have direct access to witnesses, as long as the witnesses are not compelled to speak to counsel if they do not wish to and are not represented by counsel. Here, Clarence does not appear to have counsel and he was willing to testify and assist Plaintiff's counsel. Therefore, contacting him without the Defendant's knowledge was proper. The accident scene is a public place, fully accessible by anyone, so taking Clarence there would not be improper. Taking a recorded statement would also be proper. The judge should deny the Motion for a Protective Order because Plaintiff's interview of Clarence was not unethical or privileged. Plaintiff complied with his duty to notify Defendant of the deposition time and place. Counsel should also disclose the payments made to Clarence to the Defendant. Otherwise, counsel's behavior is ethical and acceptable.

3) It is not ethical for the Defendant's attorney to subpoena a witness for a hearing without notifying opposing counsel in advance. A subpoena is not a discovery device and should not be used to conduct a "fishing expedition" into the Plaintiff's background. If the transcript is relevant to the Defendant's case (which it could be, depending on Arthur's disability) or could produce relevant evidence in discovery, the Defendant should properly request these documents in discovery rather than using a subpoena. Furthermore, the subpoena was improper because it did not reference a valid proceeding. The court would not have the authority to exercise the subpoena without an appropriate proceeding. Plaintiff could move to quash the subpoena or the information discovered in the subpoena if the registrar complied with the subpoena without Plaintiff's knowledge. If the registrar complies with the subpoena and sends the transcript to the Defendant, the plaintiff could prevent disclosure of the evidence

through a motion in limine to exclude the evidence, based on a rule of evidence, such as irrelevance or its relevance is substantially outweighed by the danger of unfair prejudice. Some hearsay rules may also apply, although the transcript is probably admissible as a business record.

QUESTION #4 (SAMPLE 3) 820 words

1) Plaintiff's counsel did not breach any ethical duties or standards by filing the complaint for damages prior to having conducted any investigation into the facts. In this case, the statute of limitations was about to run and the attorney had only two days in which to file a complaint. Attorney did not file the complaint without any investigation or actual knowledge of the facts, instead, he did have some knowledge of the incident, which he gathered by reviewing the accident report. There is no requirement that an attorney must conduct a full-fledged investigation before they file a complaint, although ideally that is the course that an attorney would like to follow. Here, there simply wasn't enough time to conduct additional investigation other than to read the accident report and file a complaint. When an attorney files a complaint in GA, they sign it and simply affirm that it is not being brought for any improper purpose. And that requirement is met here. The attorney was not filling the complaint for any improper purpose. It should be noted that in GA even though the attorney is required to sign the complaint and aver to certain things, there is no mention of any particular sanctions if an attorney were found to have violated this rule. This is very different from the Federal rules, which are very specific as to what the attorney is swearing to when he signs the complaint and provided detailed sanctions which are often enforced if an attorney is found to have violated the federal rule. Furthermore, if the attorney is concerned about his actions in filing the complaint without having the opportunity to conduct additional investigation, he could always file an amended complaint as soon as possible as a matter of right anytime before trial, or attorney could voluntarily dismiss the case (with Arthur's guardian's consent) prior to the defendant answering and then under Georgia's renewal statute the attorney would have the remaining statute of limitations period or six months, whichever is longer, to refile as a matter of right. This means that even though the statute of limitations period had run in this case, attorney would still have six months to re-file and the dismissal of the previous claim could not be used against the plaintiff in the second case.
   Regardless of which avenue counsel takes, he has an obligation to be a zealous advocate for his client and has a continuing obligation to conduct a proper investigation on behalf of his client. Counsel also has a duty of candor to the court, which means he has a duty to be honest and forthright with the tribunal at all times.
2) I believe that under GA law, the court should deny the protective order. Unlike in federal court, in GA there are no initial mandatory disclosures, such as people who may have relevant information about the crime. Both counsels have a right to track down witnesses, interview them, collect information, revisit the accident scene, etc.

without contacting the other side before hand, unless the person being interviewed etc is the opposing party, in which case counsel's permission is required. This is all part of the investigation of a client's case. More formal inquires such as depositions do require that you notify the other party, which counsel did prior to taking Clarence's deposition. Additionally, it does not appear that plaintiff's attorney was trying to pull a fast one on the defense because defense counsel knew that plaintiff's attorney was looking for Clarence, since plaintiff's attorney had contacted the defense about Clarence's location, and plaintiff's attorney did notify the defense that it had located Clarence and provided the defense with his location, as well as noticing their deposition, thus defense was not prejudiced by the plaintiff's counsel's actions and has an equal opportunity to investigate the matter themselves. Therefore, there is no reason to grant the protective order. This would be a different answer if Clarence had still been an employee of Hauling Freight, in which case, plaintiff's counsel would have had to notify Hauling prior to flying Clarence out and interviewing him because Hauling is a defendant and Clarence as an employee would have been considered an agent of Hauling. However, since Clarence was fired for reasons unrelated to the accident, I do not believe that the plaintiff's counsel had to notify defense counsel before it took any of the actions it did. Therefore, I think that the protective order should be denied. Even if the protective order is granted by the court and Clarence's prior recorded statement is excluded, there is nothing to prevent the P's counsel from gathering the same information through the deposition or from calling Clarence as a witness at trial.

3) Here, defense counsel has probably violated some ethical rules by failing to notify plaintiff's counsel of the subpoena of the registrar and for subpoenaing the registrar for a non-existing hearing. The plaintiff is entitled to notice of subpoenas in a case, particularly when it is a subpoena for an alleged hearing and requesting that a non-party produce certain documents. Additionally, the fact that defense counsel knows that the subpoena is for a non-existent hearing is violative of the attorney's ethical obligations. This is taking action for an improper purpose and also violates the duty of candor. If all the defendant wants is to get the documents then all the defense had to do in GA would be to file a request for production of documents with the non-party, a subpoena is not required in GA.

Assuming that the registrar produced the transcript at or before the non-existent hearing, plaintiff's counsel could file a motion exclude the evidence or a protective order due to the defense counsel's violations in order to ensure that the defendant does not gain some unfair advantage by acting unethically. In the alternative, plaintiff's counsel could seek to have the transcripts turned over to them immediately as well. It is unclear what relevance Arthur's college transcripts have in this case, so it is possible that plaintiff's counsel will not want to bother with the process of trying to have the evidence excluded or otherwise limited in use.

In addition to trying to get the transcripts kicked out, plaintiff's counsel should report the defense counsel to the Georgia Bar for his ethical violations and abuse of the process.

JULY 2016 BAR EXAMINATION

QUESTION #1

On October 11, 2015, State's Witness went to the Fulton County home of his friend, Victim 1, and parked behind an unfamiliar car in the driveway, a maroon Toyota Camry. A man was sitting in the passenger's seat. State's Witness knocked on the door of the house and rang the doorbell, but no one answered. Then as he began to back his car out of the driveway, he saw a man with "blondish colored hair" walking from behind Victim 1's garage. State's Witness pulled back into the driveway and asked the man what he was doing. The man told him that his car was running hot and they were looking for water, but when they stopped the car, their dog, a black and white terrier, jumped out of the car window, and they were looking for it. State's Witness wrote down the car's license tag number, told the men to leave, and then notified the police and Victim 1.

An officer from the Fulton County Police Department responded to the call, but found nothing suspicious. Victim 1 did not notice anything missing until approximately one month later when she noticed that jewelry she kept in a box was missing.

The license plate number that State's Witness wrote down was later traced back to Defendant's mother. At trial, Co-Defendant testified that he was the man sitting in the passenger's seat of that car when State's Witness arrived, and Defendant was the man who emerged from behind the garage to speak with State's Witness. Co-Defendant said that Defendant had entered Victim 1's house while he sat outside, and when Defendant got back in the car, he pulled a bundle of gold jewelry out of his pocket. The men sold some of the jewelry for cash that same day.

Nine days after the incident at Victim 1's house, Victim 2 went to her Fulton County home during her lunch break. When she arrived, she saw a "reddish burgundy" car, with the hood up, parked in her carport next to her water spigot. A dark-haired man of average height was looking under the hood, and as she pulled in the driveway, he approached her car to tell her that he had stopped to get some water because his car had been running hot. Victim 2 then noticed a man inside her house through the kitchen window. As she began backing out of her driveway, the dark-haired man said their dog had jumped out of the car window and the other man was looking for it. As Victim 2 called 911, she saw the other man come around the front of her house; Victim 2 described him as blonde and a little older and taller than the first man. As she was talking on the phone, the men pulled up beside her. The blonde man told her that they did not mean to scare her, but Victim 2 told him that she had seen him inside her house. The man denied it and then drove off.

Co-Defendant testified at trial that Defendant and he were the men at Victim 2's home that day, and Defendant was driving the same Toyota Camry he drove to Victim 1's house. Co-Defendant was the man outside under the hood of the car when Victim 2 drove up, and Defendant was inside the house. He said that Defendant had only been in the house a couple of minutes when Victim 2 arrived.

Co-Defendant further testified that Defendant and he committed burglaries to get money to buy drugs. Co-Defendant joined Defendant for the first time on the burglary of Victim 1's house. He said that Defendant usually drove the maroon Toyota Camry, picked out the locations for the burglaries, and broke into the houses using a plastic credit card to manipulate the locks, while Co-Defendant waited outside. After the burglaries, they sold the stolen valuables for cash.

DeKalb County Investigator testified that Co-Defendant was arrested first in connection with two unrelated DeKalb County burglaries. Afterwards, he cooperated with the DeKalb County Police Department by showing investigators the residences he had burglarized alone, residences he had burglarized with Defendant, and residences he said Defendant had identified as places he had burglarized alone in Fulton, DeKalb, and Clayton Counties. During the investigation into these burglaries, an investigator discovered that Defendant had pawned a Decatur High School class ring ("Class Ring"), belonging to Victim 3, who lived at one of the sites that Co-Defendant claimed Defendant had admitted burglarizing alone ("Victim 3 burglary"). The State presented evidence of Defendant's arrest in connection with this third burglary, which took place in DeKalb County. The State introduced a copy of the pawn ticket ("Pawn Ticket"), for the ring, which contained Defendant's name and identifying information.

At trial, Defendant's attorney led off his cross-examination of Co-Defendant by questioning his motives for testifying and attacked his credibility throughout the trial. Defendant's attorney elicited testimony that Co-Defendant had rejected a plea deal with the hope that the State would offer a better one if he cooperated and testified at Defendant's trial.

The trial court received the jury's verdicts of guilty, and deferred sentencing until a pre-sentence report could be presented and considered. At the sentencing hearing the trial judge expressed strong negative opinions about the moral character of the Defendant as demonstrated by the witnesses who testified at trial.

The Defendant was sentenced to serve a period of years in prison. Thereafter, the Defendant's trial counsel filed a Motion for New Trial and moved to recuse the trial judge from consideration of the Motion for New Trial based upon her expressed bias against Defendant evidenced by her negative and personal comments during sentencing about his lack of moral character. The Motion to Recuse was supported by an affidavit signed and sworn to by the Defendant. The trial judge dismissed the Motion to Recuse for failing to state a claim for recusal and proceeded one week later to hear and deny the Motion for New Trial.

Your senior partner has been appointed as appellate counsel and has asked you to prepare a memorandum analyzing three issues.

Questions:
1. Whether evidence of "other acts" was properly admitted into evidence?
2. Whether the DeKalb County investigator's testimony of prior statements made by Co-Defendant regarding Victim 3 burglary were properly admitted into evidence?
3. Whether the trial judge's dismissal of the Motion to Recuse was proper?

QUESTION #2

On a whim, and fueled by alcohol, Defendants Butch and Shane left Atlanta at approximately 10:00 p.m. headed to Florida in Butch's burgundy Lincoln. Their trip was spontaneous, so they had virtually no money or extra clothing. An hour or so south of Atlanta they pulled into a public rest area on I-75 in Monroe County. Wearing his Army field jacket and a Pittsburgh Pirates ball cap, Shane entered the men's restroom armed with a .38 revolver and robbed Victim A of his wallet and $77.00 in cash (3 twenties, 3 fives and 2 ones).

With Butch at the wheel, he and Shane fled down I-75 hoping to get more money and some extra clothes. Twenty minutes later and on the north side of Macon, they pulled into the parking lot of a chain hotel. Butch got out and Shane took his place at the wheel. Butch put on Shane's field jacket and Pirates cap and, with his .32 pistol in the jacket pocket, he entered the hotel and went to the 4th floor looking for an occupied room. Finding one, he knocked and announced "Room Service" loudly. Victim B, a North Carolina electrician working on a project in Macon and sharing a room with fellow employee, Victim C, opened the door leaving the chain in place. Butch kicked the door open and entered with pistol drawn, firing a bullet into the headboard next to Victim C. After gathering wallets, watches, cash, shirts and pants, Butch threatened to kill them if they opened the door. He then fled the hotel and parking lot with Shane driving the Lincoln.

The rest stop crime was reported immediately by Victim A to the Monroe County Sheriff who issued a "Be On Look Out" (BOLO) to law enforcement throughout Middle Georgia about the incident and gave a description of the car, the field jacket and ball cap. Shortly after the hotel incident, a Bibb County deputy saw a car matching the Monroe County description, swerving and speeding on I-75. He then called for back-up, and pulled Shane and Butch over.

As Shane and Butch were being questioned, a deputy saw through the rear window a ball cap in the back seat matching the BOLO description previously given. A field jacket was also seen wadded up on the rear floorboard. After being formally charged and arrested, Butch was searched by officers who found the wallets of Victims B and C in his pants. Shane was then searched, and $77.00 in cash, consisting of 3 twenties, 3 fives and 2 ones, was found in his pocket. Although Shane did not own the car, Shane agreed to a search of the trunk of Butch's car where the clothing of Victims B and C were found along with Victim A's wallet. A search of the interior of the Lincoln by officers led to the discovery of a .38 revolver in the glove compartment and a .32 pistol in the console between the driver and the passenger seats.

Questions:
1. With what major felony crimes, and in what county or counties, would Butch and Shane likely be indicted?
2. If defense counsel later filed a motion to suppress the evidence seized from the persons of Butch and Shane, as well as from the Lincoln, how should the state justify the warrantless search and seizure of the various items of evidence?
3. After their arrests, Butch and Shane were taken to the hotel. There Victims B and C were brought down from their room to the patrol car, and they identified Butch as their assailant. At the time of identification, Butch was seated in the back seat with Shane and both were in handcuffs. If Butch's attorney later moved to suppress the "show up" identification as evidence, what would be the basis for the motion, what would be the state's likely response, and what would be the likely ruling?

QUESTION #3

Sister and brother, Laura and Sam Smith, inherited a five-acre lakefront property located on Lake Oconee (the "Smith Property") from their mother who died in 2005. The devise in the mother's Will reads as follows: "I leave my Lake Oconee property to my children, Sam and Laura." Their father had predeceased their mother, and Sam and Laura were Mrs. Smith's only heirs. In addition to a large six-bedroom house, the Smith Property also has a pool, a small private lake and direct access to Lake Oconee.

For several years following Mrs. Smith's death, Sam and Laura and their families used the Smith Property as a retreat, either together or as separate family units throughout the year. The Smith Property was well-maintained, with both Sam and Laura contributing equally to the upkeep and maintenance.

In 2010, Laura and her family relocated to Key West, Florida. Thereafter, Laura and her family did not travel back to Georgia to use the lake house. In 2011, Sam and his wife divorced. Sam found it more and more difficult to spend time at the lake house. Sam told Laura that there were too many memories at the lake house and he would rather be anywhere other than there.

In 2009, Nell and Jeff Jones had purchased property (the "Jones Property") immediately adjacent to the Smith Property. The Jones Property consisted of one acre with a very large house. It was not a lakefront tract and had no pool or private lake. Prior to Laura's relocation and Sam's divorce, the Joneses often visited with Sam and his family at the Smith Property and enjoyed using the pool and the private lake. The Joneses also used a portion of the Smith Property as a shortcut to Lake Oconee since the Jones Property had no lake frontage of its own.

When Sam divorced, he told the Joneses that they should feel free to use the pool, fish in the private lake, and to cut through the Smith Property to reach Lake Oconee. In 2013, the Joneses decided to turn the Jones Property into a bed and breakfast. They were enthusiastic about this because their guests could use the pool and fish in the private lake on the Smith Property. Their guests could also use the shortcut over the Smith Property for direct access to Lake Oconee.

Because neither he nor Laura and her family were going to be using the Smith Property as they had in the past, Sam decided that he would rent out the Smith Property. Sam did not notify Laura of his rental idea. From 2011 through the summer of 2014, Sam regularly rented the Smith Property on a weekly or sometimes monthly basis. He did not share any of the profits from the rentals with Laura. Sam merely reported to Laura that everything was fine, and Laura continued to pay her share of the expenses for maintenance and upkeep of the Smith Property.

In 2015, a hotel company offered to purchase the Smith Property. It was just the right size for a new boutique hotel. Sam and Laura were happy to sell the Smith Property since neither of them personally used it anymore and the purchase price offered by the hotel company was well above market value.

The Joneses learned of the pending sale when Sam visited the Smith Property to pack up the furnishings and personal belongings in the house. During this visit, Sam told the Joneses that they would no longer be able to use the pool, the private lake, or the shortcut to Lake Oconee located on the Smith Property. The Joneses were furious since they were counting on these Smith Property amenities as part of the attraction of their bed and breakfast retreat. The Joneses told Sam that they planned to notify the hotel company that they had easement rights in the Smith Property.

Sam is worried because he wants to sell the Smith Property. He is unsure what rights, if any, the Joneses have in the Smith Property. He is also concerned that Laura will find out that he has been renting the Smith Property without her knowledge for several years. Sam has come to your firm for advice regarding his situation. Your senior partner would like for you to address the following questions in a detailed memo:

Questions:
1. When Mrs. Smith left the lake property to Laura and Sam, what ownership interest was created pursuant to the devise in her Will? Please fully explain your answer.
2. What property rights or interests do the Joneses have in the Smith Property? Please

fully explain your answer.

3. Is Sam obligated to pay Laura any portion of the rents that Sam collected from the weekly and monthly rentals of the Smith Property? If so, to how much is Laura entitled?

4. Assuming the sale of the Smith Property is consummated, to how much of the net proceeds is Sam entitled? Please explain.

QUESTION #4

John is the owner of Artists of Augusta, a magazine directed at art collectors and enthusiasts. John would like to win the "Meilleure Peinture," a nationwide competition that gives an award and a $1,000,000 cash prize to the magazine featuring the rarest and best painting each year. John is convinced that if he wins this award, his magazine circulation will increase dramatically and he will attract additional advertisers. The competition is scheduled to begin on October 1. The entry applications are due by September 1.

John has discovered a long lost painting by Ginger, a world-renowned oil painter who is deceased. This discovery will shock the art world, as it has not previously been catalogued or referenced. If John can get the painting, he has a good chance of winning the coveted "Meilleure Peinture."

The painting is owned by Bill. On July 1, John and Bill entered into a valid, written contract. Bill agreed to sell and John agreed to buy the painting for $500,000. The painting was to be delivered to John by September 14. Assuming that he would obtain the painting, John signed up for the "Meilleure Peinture" competition, which required a non-refundable entry fee of $10,000.

On September 4, Bill told John that he had just sold the painting for $750,000 to Frenchie, and he would deliver the painting to a shipping company to get it to Frenchie within one week.

Questions:

1. What remedies are available to prevent Bill from delivering the painting to the shipping company? Include in your answer the grounds and procedures for obtaining this relief.

2. What remedies are available to force Bill to honor the sales contract? Include in your answer the grounds and procedures for obtaining this relief.

3. What damages, if any, can John reasonably recover from Bill? Explain your answer.

4. In which court(s) may John seek the above relief?

5. Assume John files an action seeking all forms of relief identified in your responses to questions 2 and 3, above. What form(s) of relief, if any, is the Court likely to grant? Explain your answer.

JULY 2016 BAR EXAMINATION ANSWERS

> These "model" answers have been prepared and edited for the limited purpose of illustrating the writing style and the fact, law, application methodology taught in the Essay Writing Workshop. You should not rely on these answers for accurate black letter law. The writer's analysis and conclusions are not the only way to approach these essays, and keep in mind that these "models" do not represent perfect answers, but rather acceptable passing essays.

MODEL ANSWER TO QUESTION #1

I.   Other Acts

At trial, DeKalb County Investigator testified that Co-Defendant was arrested first in connection with two unrelated DeKalb County burglaries. Then the State presented evidence of Defendant's arrest in connection with this third burglary, which took place in DeKalb County.

Defendant will argue that any past burglaries do not speak to any relevant issue regarding this charge and that this evidence is inadmissible to prove he is a burglar by nature. The prosecution may not introduce character evidence to show that the criminal defendant was the kind of person likely to commit a crime. The state will respond that the evidence was properly admitted because the prior burglaries show that Defendant knows how to commit a burglary and has done it before, therefore, it may be admitted. Proof that a criminal defendant has committed other crimes is admissible if offered to show motive, opportunity, intent, preparation, plan, knowledge, identity, or absence of mistake or accident.

The state will win its argument because the evidence was offered to show identity and plan. Here, the evidence of Co-Defendant's prior arrests is offered to show the identity of the Defendant and Co-Defendant, as well as a common plan among all the crimes. The previous burglaries included men who were parked close to the house in a car described as maroon and "reddish burgundy," which shows identity. In addition, both of the previous burglaries included a statement to police stating that the occupants of the car said that their car was running hot and they were looking for water, which shows a common plan among the crimes. Further, the previous burglaries also included statements to police that the man at the scene had "blondish colored hair," which also goes to identity. Therefore, the admission of other acts was proper in this case.

II.   Co-Defendant Testimony

Co-Defendant cooperated with the DeKalb County Police Department by showing investigators the residences he had burglarized alone, residences he had burglarized with Defendant, and residences he said Defendant had identified as places he had burglarized alone in Fulton, DeKalb, and Clayton Counties.

Defendant will argue that the statements made by him to Co-Defendant are hearsay without any exception, because they are all out of court statements used to prove the truth of what was said. Hearsay is an out of court statement offered for the truth of the matter asserted. The state will argue however, that the Defendant's statement to Co-Defendant falls within an exception to the hearsay rule as an admission by a party opponent. An admission by a party opponent is an exception to the hearsay rule. Defendant will argue that, notwithstanding, statements from Co- Defendant to Investigator are hearsay not within any exception. The state will reply that the testimony falls within an exception to the hearsay rule as statements were made to co-defendant in furtherance of a conspiracy. Statements made by co-conspirators during the course and in furtherance of the conspiracy are exceptions to hearsay.

The state will win its argument that statements made to Co-Defendant that Defendant had committed a burglary alone at the location of Victim 3's burglary, are an admission by a party opponent. Generally, an out of court statement offered to prove the truth of the matter asserted is not allowed under the hearsay rule. However, if a party to the action is the one making the out of court statement, it will be admitted. Here, Defendant told the Co-Defendant that he had independently burglarized Victim 3's house. Therefore, since Defendant is a party to the action, his statement to Co-Defendant was properly admitted. Defendant will however win his argument excluding Investigator's testimony regarding Victim 3's burglary because it is hearsay within hearsay not within any exception. Here, the Co-Defendant made statements to the Investigator about statements that Defendant made to him. The state will fail in its argument that the statement is one of a co-conspirator because it was not made in furtherance of the crime, but was made after Co-Defendant was arrested. The rule states that an out-of court-statement made by one conspirator after he has been arrested, implicating the other conspirators, is not admissible against them. Therefore, the Co-Defendant's statement to the Investigator about the Victim 3 burglary was improperly admitted at trial.

III.   Motion to Recuse

The Defendant's trial counsel filed a Motion for New Trial and moved to recuse the trial judge from consideration of the Motion for New Trial based upon her expressed bias against Defendant evidenced by her negative and personal comments during sentencing about his lack of moral character. The trial judge dismissed the Motion to Recuse for failing to state a claim for recusal and proceeded one week later to hear and deny the Motion for New Trial.

Defendant will argue that the denial of the recusal and the judge's ruling on the motion for new trial was improper because of her statements impugning his character. A judge must recuse herself where she has a personal bias or prejudice concerning a party. The state will respond that the denial of the recusal was proper because they came after the trial was over. A judge is not required to recuse herself unless her bias and prejudice would result in an unfair trial for the Defendant.

The state will win its argument because the judge's denial of the Motion to Recuse was proper. A judge must recuse herself if she has a personal bias or prejudice against a party. Here, the judge expressed strong negative opinions about the moral character of the Defendant based on what she had heard at trial from the witnesses. Although the judge did express strong negative opinions, these statements were made after the jury came to a verdict and had been dismissed. There are no facts available to show that the judge held these opinions before or during the trial, or that they prejudiced Defendant in any way. Therefore, the judge's denial of the Motion to Recuse was proper because it did not state a claim for recusal.

MODEL ANSWER TO QUESTION #2

I.   Felonies

A. Shane

In Monroe County, Shane entered the men's restroom armed with a .38 revolver and robbed Victim A of his wallet and $77.00 in cash (three twenties, three fives and two ones). Shane also drove the car after Butch entered into Victim B and C's Macon hotel and stole their wallets, watches, cash, shirts, and pants. They were arrested in Bib County.

i.   Armed Robbery

The state will argue that Shane should be indicted in Monroe County for armed robbery. One who uses an offensive weapon and thereby takes property from the person of another with the intent to commit theft is guilty of the felony of armed robbery. Shane will argue that he was intoxicated at the time of the alleged robbery. Voluntary intoxication is not an excuse for any criminal act or omission to act.

The state will be successful in its indictment of Shane because he committed the felony of armed robbery. Here, Shane entered a men's restroom armed with a .38 revolver, an offensive weapon and took property, a wallet, and $77.00 in cash from Victim A. Shane's defense of intoxication will be unsuccessful because the facts indicate that the intoxication was voluntary and therefore not a defense to the aggravated assault indictment. Therefore, Shane can be indicted for armed robbery in Monroe County, where the crime took place.

    ii.   Accessory After the Fact

The state will argue that Shane was an accessory after the fact for Butch's crimes. An accessory after the fact assists the principal in aiding him in his escape. Shane will argue that he didn't know that Butch intended to rob Victim B and C in their hotel room. An accessory must have knowledge of the commission of a felony.

The state will be successful in its indictment of Shane because he is an accessory after the fact for Butch's crimes (described below). Shane saw Butch get out of the car with his field jacket and Pirates cap. Shane will unsuccessfully argue that he didn't know that Butch was going to rob anyone. Although Shane could not see Butch's gun because it was in his pocket, the facts indicate that the two fled the scene of Shane's robbery hoping to get more cash and clothes. Shane was an accessory after the fact when he drove the car away from the hotel where Butch robbed Victim B and C. Therefore, Shane can be indicted for an accessory after the fact to Butch's crimes in Bibb County because that is where Butch's crimes took place.

    B. Butch

In Bibb County, Butch kicked opened Victim B and C's hotel door and entered with pistol drawn, firing a bullet into the headboard next to Victim C. After gathering wallets, watches, cash, shirts, and pants, Butch threatened to kill them if they opened the door. Shane drove the car away from the scene.

    i.   Burglary

The state will argue that Butch should be indicted for the felony of burglary. A person without authority and with the intent to commit a felony who enters or remains in the dwelling of another (including a hotel room) commits burglary in the first degree. Butch will argue that he did not have the intent to rob Victims B and C before he entered the hotel room. To convict for the crime of burglary, it must be shown that at the time he breaks and enters the dwelling of another, the defendant intends to commit a felony which is causally connected with his breaking and entering.

The state will be successful in its indictment of Butch for burglary. Here, Butch left his car wearing Shane's clothing (the same worn in the robbery twenty minutes before) with a gun in his pocket. He sought out an occupied room on the 4th floor with the intent to steal more money and extra clothes. Butch broke into a hotel room by kicking the door down, entered with gun drawn showing an intent to rob the occupants. He then took Victim B and C's wallets, watches, cash, shirts, and pants. Therefore, Butch can be indicted for burglary in Bibb County because that is where the burglary took place.

ii. Aggravated Assault

The state will argue that it can indict Butch for the felony of aggravated assault. Aggravated assault is the attempt to commit violent injury to another or the commission of acts which place another in reasonable apprehension of immediate violent injury with use of a deadly weapon. Butch will argue that he did not intend to rob Victims B and C. Aggravated assault may also be proven by showing the Defendant's intent to rob or murder the victims.

The state will be successful in its indictment of Butch for aggravated assault because he fired a bullet into the headboard next to Victim C. Here, Victim C had reasonable apprehension of immediate injury because of the proximity of the bullet to his person. In addition, Victims B and C were apprehensive of further injury based on Butch's threat to kill them if they opened the door after he left. Therefore, the state can bring an indictment for aggravated assault against Butch in Bibb County because that is where the incident took place.

iii. Accessory After the Fact

The state will argue that Butch was an accessory after the fact for Shane's crime. An accessory after the fact assists the principal in aiding him in his escape. Butch will argue that he didn't know that Shane intended to rob Victim A at the rest stop. An accessory must have knowledge of the commission of a felony.

The state will be successful in its indictment of Butch because he is an accessory after the fact for Shane's crimes (described above). Butch will unsuccessfully argue that he didn't know that Shane was going to rob anyone. However, Butch saw Shane get back in the car with Victim A's wallet and they fled hoping the get more money and some extra clothes. Butch can therefore be indicted as an accessory after the fact to Shane's crimes in Monroe County because that is where Shane's crimes took place.

II. Motion to Suppress Evidence

A. Ball Cap

The police officer saw a Pirates baseball cap through the rear window the Lincoln after Shane and Butch were pulled over for matching the description of the BOLO and swerving and speeding on I-75.

The state will argue that the baseball cap should not be excluded because it was in plain view of the officer. An exception to the warrant requirement is if an officer sees potential evidence in plain view. Shane and Butch will argue that the baseball cap should be excluded because the stop was invalid. In order to use the plain view exception, the officer must show that he had probable cause to stop the car.

The state will be successful in justifying the warrantless search with regards to the baseball cap. Here, a BOLO was issued describing the Defendants' car, the field jacket, and the baseball cap. Further, Shane was swerving and speeding down I-75 when officers spotted the car. Probable cause is met under these facts. Therefore, when the officer was questioning Butch and Shane and saw the baseball cap, it was within the plain view exception to collect the baseball cap for evidence without a warrant.

B. Cash and Wallets of Victims B and C

After being formally charged and arrested, Butch was searched by officers who found the wallets of Victims B and C in his pants. Shane was then searched, and $77.00 in cash, consisting of three twenties, three fives and two ones, was found in his pocket.

The state will argue that these items were lawfully obtained under the search incident to lawful arrest exception to the warrant requirement. A warrantless search is valid if it is reasonable in scope. Butch and Shane will again argue that the arrest was not lawful. A warrantless search must also be made incident to a lawful arrest.

The state will be successful in justifying the warrantless search of both Shane and Butch under the search incident to lawful arrest exception. Here, Shane and Butch were stopped based on the officer's probable cause that the car matched the BOLO and they found the baseball cap in the back of the Lincoln when they were questioning Butch and Shane. Finding the baseball cap gave the police probable cause to arrest Butch and Shane on suspicion of committing the crimes described above. The officers had the right to search Butch and Shane for evidence and to ensure the officers safety in case the defendants had weapons. Therefore, the discovery of Victim B and C's wallets and the cash, in the same denominations that were stolen from Victim A would not be suppressed based on the warrantless search.

C. Clothing of Victims B & C and Victim A's Wallet

Although Shane did not own the car, Shane agreed to a search of the trunk of Butch's car where the clothing of Victims B and C were found along with Victim A's wallet.

The state will argue that the search of the trunk that revealed the clothing was justified without a warrant because Shane consented to the search. A person's voluntarily consent to a search is an exception to the warrant requirement. Butch will argue that Shane did not have the right to consent to the search because it was Butch's car. In the absence of the defendant, a third party may consent to search areas that are under joint control, but not where another person has exclusive control.

The state will be successful in its argument that the police were justified in searching the trunk based on Shane's consent. Here, Shane was driving the car when the police officers pulled them over for swerving and speeding (also for matching the BOLO). It was reasonable that the officers would believe that Shane had the authority to consent to the search of the trunk. Further, Butch was not absent at the time of consent and could have told the officers it was his car, not Shane's. Therefore, the items collected from the trunk would be admissible and the state would be successful in arguing that the police were justified in searching the trunk without a warrant based on consent.

D. Revolver and Pistol

A search of the interior of the Lincoln by officers led to the discovery of a .38 revolver in the glove compartment and a .32 pistol in the console between the driver and the passenger seats.

The state will argue that it was justified in collecting the revolver and the pistol under the automobile exception to the warrant requirement. If there is probable cause, the police may conduct a warrantless search of every part of the vehicle and its contents, including all containers and packages that may conceal the object of the search. Butch and Shane will argue that the evidence should be suppressed because the officers did not have probable cause to search the car. The automobile exception applies when there is probable cause to search the automobile.

The state will be successful in justifying the collection of the revolver and the pistol from the interior of the car under the automobile exception. Here, the officers had probable cause to search the entire car because they had already found the baseball cap, the wallets and clothing of Victim B and C, and the cash and wallet of Victim A. Further, Victim A had reported that he was held at gunpoint at the rest area. The police had reason to believe that the guns used in the robberies was in the car since they had not found it on Shane or Butch. Therefore, the police officers' search of the glove compartment and the console that uncovered the revolver and the pistol was within the automobile exception and will be justified against any suppression attack by the defense.

E. Motion to Suppress Show-Up Identification

After their arrests, Butch and Shane were taken to the hotel. There Victims B and C were brought down from their room to the patrol car, and they identified Butch as their assailant. At the time of identification, Butch was seated in the back seat with Shane and both were in handcuffs.

The state will argue that the identification was valid because it was necessary to know whether the police needed to go out and pursue different men for these crimes. A show-up identification made near the scene and time of the crime can be necessary if it helps the police determine if the person captured is actually the criminal. Butch and Shane will argue that the show-up line-up was invalid because it was suggestive of their guilt. Due process is violated if the show-up identification is unnecessarily suggestive and conducive to irreparable mistaken identification.

The state will be successful in arguing a denial of the defendant's Motion to Suppress the show-up identification if it can show that it was necessary to show Butch and Shane to the victims immediately after their arrest. Here, the police had reports of two men that had committed two armed robberies in the space of an hour. Once arrested, if the police can prove to the court that the immediate identification was necessary to know whether they had the right men or whether they needed to continue looking, then the show-up identification may be allowed in court. However, the defendants also have a good argument that the show-up identification should be suppressed because it violated their due process rights by being overly suggestive. Here, the show-up took place while Butch and Shane were handcuffed in the backseat of a police car. Therefore, the judge has the obligation to weigh the need of the police to catch the suspects for public safety and the defendants' rights to due process in the show-up identification.

MODEL ANSWER TO QUESTION #3

I.   Laura and Sam's Interest Through Devise

Laura and Sam inherited the Smith property through a devise in the mother's will, which read as follows: "I leave my Lake Oconee property to my children, Sam and Laura." Sam and Laura were Mrs. Smith's only heirs. In addition to a large six-bedroom house, the Smith Property also has a pool, a small private lake, and direct access to Lake Oconee.

Laura will argue that they own the property as joint tenants with right to survivorship. Joint tenants own the properly jointly and receive the others' interest upon death if a right to survivorship is clearly stated. Sam will argue that they own the property as tenants in common. Tenants in common hold property in equal shares unless stated otherwise.

Sam will win his argument that he owns the Smith property as a tenant in common with his sister, Laura. Here, Laura and Sam's mother devises the Smith Property through her will, stating "I leave my Lake Oconee property to my children, Sam and Laura." Laura's joint tenancy argument fails because there is no language in the devise for a joint tenancy or right of survivorship. Without this language, the devise of the property creates a tenancy in common. Therefore, Sam and Laura own the Smith property in equal shares and each has the ability to convey or devise their one-half interest in the property.

II.   Joneses' Interest

Nell and Jeff Jones own a property adjacent to the Smith Property. The Joneses visited Laura and Sam, used the pool, and accessed the lake. When Sam divorced, he told the Joneses that they should feel free to use the pool, fish in the private lake, and to cut through the Smith Property to reach Lake Oconee. Due to the use of the pool and access to the lake, the Joneses decide to open a bed and breakfast.

Sam will argue that he gave Nell and Jeff Jones a license to use the pool, fish in the private lake, and to access Lake Oconee, therefore the Joneses had no easement rights in the Smith Property. A license is a right given by the owner that permits a person to go onto and use the owner's land. The Joneses will argue that they have a prescriptive easement to use the pool and access the lake. A prescriptive easement is created when there is actual use, and that use is open and notorious, continuous, and adverse.

Sam will be successful in his argument that the Joneses had a license to use the pool and access the lake via the Smith Property. Here, Sam told the Joneses that they should feel free to use the pool, fish in the private lake, and to cut through the Smith Property to reach Lake Oconee. The Joneses did not give value for this right and therefore the license is revocable by Sam at any time, which he did when he sold the property to the hotel company in 2015. The Joneses' argument that they hold an easement to the property fails because (1) the easement was not in writing and (2) they do not meet the required elements for a prescriptive easement. Under the Statute of Frauds, a conveyance in land must be in writing to be valid. Here, Sam's permission for the use of the Smith property was oral. Further, the Joneses fail to show a prescriptive easement because although they used the land, open and notoriously and continuously, it was not adverse because Sam gave his permission for their use and access to the Smith Property. Therefore, the Joneses have no easement, nor any other ownership interest in the Smith Property.

III.   Obligation to Laura for Rents

Sam decided that he would rent out the Smith Property. Sam did not notify Laura of his rental idea. From 2011 through the summer of 2014, Sam regularly rented the Smith Property on a weekly or sometimes monthly basis. He did not share any of the profits from the rentals with Laura. Laura continued to pay her share of the expenses for maintenance and upkeep of the Smith Property.

Sam will argue that he should not have to give Laura any of the rents because she moved away and left him with all the responsibilities of the Smith Property. If one cotenant receives rent from third persons, he is liable to account for the net proceeds received, but would be entitled to deduct operating expenses such as taxes, mortgages, interest, and management. Laura will argue that she continued to pay her share of the expenses for maintenance and upkeep of the Smith Property and should receive half of the rent amounts. Cotenants who pay their share of the expenses for maintenance and upkeep are entitled to their share of any rent received by third parties.

Laura will be successful in showing that she is entitled to half of the rents collected from 2011 to 2014 less any taxes, mortgages, interest, or management costs that Sam incurred. Here, although she moved away, Laura continued to uphold her obligations by paying her share of expenses. As a cotenant, she is entitled to half of the rents collected by Sam from 2011 and 2014 due to her interest in the property. Sam will lose his argument that he should not have to pay Laura any of the rents because she lived out of state and he was managing the property. As stated above, Sam has the right to deduct for any management expenses, but he must give the remainder of the money he collected for rent between 2011 to 2014 to Laura because she is a cotenant.

IV.   Sam's Net Proceeds After Sale

In 2015, a hotel company offered to purchase the Smith Property. It was just the right size for a new boutique hotel. Sam and Laura were happy to sell the Smith Property since neither of them personally used it anymore and the purchase price offered by the hotel company was well above market value.

Sam will argue that he should receive half of the proceeds from the sale of the Smith Property. A cotenant is entitled to an equal share of the proceeds when a property is sold. Laura will argue that Sam's proceeds should be deducted by the amount he owes her for the rent amounts either willingly or through a constructive trust. A constructive trust is an equitable remedy used to avoid unjust enrichment of one party at the expense of another where legal title to property was obtained either (1) by fraud, duress, or undue influence, or (2) in violation of a fiduciary or confidential relationship.

Laura will be successful in her argument that Sam should only receive his half interest minus her share of rents from 2011 to 2014 that he did not share with her. Here, Sam and Laura as cotenants who are jointly selling the Smith Property are entitled to share equally in the proceeds of the sale of that property. However, Sam withheld rental income from Laura from 2011 to 2014 and she is entitled to half of these rents minus any deductions, as discussed previously. If Sam does not willingly give her the rent amount out of his half of the proceeds, she can file an action in equity to request that the court create a constructive trust for the amount of the rents that Sam owed her from 2011 to 2014. She would be qualified for this equitable remedy because Sam owed her a fiduciary duty as a family member and he wrongfully withheld rents from her that she was legally entitled to receive as a cotenant.

MODEL ANSWER TO QUESTION #4

I.   John's Remedy to Prevent Delivery

On July 1, John and Bill entered into a valid, written contract. Bill agreed to sell and John agreed to buy a painting for $500,000. The painting was to be delivered to John by September 14. On September 4, Bill told John that he had just sold the painting for $750,000 to Frenchie, and he would deliver the painting to a shipping company to get it to Frenchie within one week.

John will argue that a temporary restraining order (TRO) is available to him under these circumstances. TROs are issued to prevent immediate harm to a party. John will also argue that a preliminary injunction is available to him. The party seeking the preliminary injunction must show (a) threat of irreparable harm, (b) a likelihood of success on the merits, and (c) that the balance of hardships favors the party seeking the injunction. Bill will argue that neither of these remedies will prevent him from shipping the painting to Frenchie. The court may order the party seeking the injunction to compensate the enjoined party from a wrongful injunction.

John will be successful in seeking a TRO to stop Bill's shipment of the painting to Frenchie. Here, John will need to submit a written request for a TRO with an affidavit stating that irreparable harm will occur before Bill could be notified. He would then need to argue that he would suffer immediate irreparable harm from Bill's sale and shipment of the painting to Frenchie. The best argument for irreparable harm is that this painting is unique and cannot be replaced because the painter is deceased. Further, if Frenchie has purchased the painting from Bill without knowledge of his contract with John, then John would not have a claim against Frenchie and would be limited to contract damages against Bill. If granted, the TRO would last for thirty days. In addition, John could request an injunction requesting that the court prohibit Bill from shipping the painting to Frenchie, which would last for the entire trial. He will be required to notify Bill of his request for the injunction. Further, he will again need to show the threat of irreparable harm (discussed above) and the likelihood of success on the merits. Here, John would need to show the court the valid sales agreement for the painting and evidence that Bill sold the painting to Frenchie and plans to ship it to him shortly. The court will then employ a balancing test to see if the person seeking the injunction will be more hurt than the person being enjoined. Therefore, it is likely that John will be granted a TRO or an injunction to stop Bill from shipping the painting to Frenchie.

II.   John's Remedy to Enforce Sales Contract

On July 1, John and Bill entered into a valid, written contract. Bill agreed to sell and John agreed to buy a painting for $500,000. The painting was to be delivered to John by September 14.

John will request that the court grant the remedy of specific performance. The plaintiff must show that (1) a contract does exist; (2) all conditions of the contract have been fulfilled or excused; (3) there is no adequate legal remedy; (4) enforcement is feasible; (5) mutuality of remedy exists; and (6) the defendant has no defenses. Bill will argue unsuccessfully that the amount that John offered in the contract is unconscionable and he can get more money from Frenchie. If the amount offered in a contract for the purchase of an item is egregious, then the court will not enforce the contract.

John will be successful in his request for specific performance because a contract exists, all contract conditions have been met, there is no adequate legal remedy, enforcement is feasible, mutuality exists, and the defendant has no defenses. Here, John can show the existence of a valid contract between himself and Bill in which Bill agrees to give him the painting and John agrees to give him $500,000. There are no facts stating that John is not able or willing to pay the contract price if the painting is surrendered to him, which would fulfill all the contract conditions. Further and most importantly, the painting is unique because it was painted by a famous, now deceased painter, making any other legal remedy besides enforcement inadequate. Enforcing the contract between the parties would be feasible for the court because if the TRO or injunction has been granted, then the painting is still in Bill's possession to give to John. Finally, Bill has no defense to John's claim because the amount John offered to pay was not unconscionable, just less than what Frenchie was willing to pay. Therefore, it is likely that John will be successful in seeking the equitable remedy of specific performance that will order Bill give him the painting for $500,000.

III.   Reliance and Expectancy Damages

On July 1, John and Bill entered into a valid, written contract. Bill agreed to sell and John agreed to buy the painting for $500,000. The painting was to be delivered to John by September 14. Assuming that he would obtain the painting, John signed up for the "Meilleure Peinture" competition, which required a non-refundable entry fee of $10,000.

John will argue that he should receive the $10,000 non-refundable fee that he submitted to enter the Meilleure Peinture contest and that she should receive damages in the amount of one million dollars and lost profits for his magazine. Reliance damages may be sought when a nonbreaching party has incurred some expense in relation to a contract which is later breached, whereas, expectancy damages put the nonbreaching party in the same position that he would have been in had the contract been performed. Bill will argue that he didn't know that John had entered the contest based on their July 1st contract and that winning the Meilleure Peinture million-dollar cash prize and increased circulation of his magazine due to winning the contest are too speculative to reward expectancy damages. Reliance damages do not require that the breaching party receive the benefit of any expenditure by the nonbreaching party. Furthermore, damages must not be speculative.

John will be successful in this argument to receive reliance damages because he relied on the contract with Bill when he entered the contest and paid a $10,000 nonrefundable fee. Here, John will be able to successfully show that he entered the contest because he would be receiving a long-lost painting from a famous, now deceased artist. This reliance is based entirely on the valid contract he entered into with Bill on July 1st. Bill's knowledge of whether John was going to enter the contest is irrelevant and not a valid defense against the reliance damages. Therefore, John will most likely receive reliance damages in the amount of $10,000. However, on the issue of expectancy damages, Bill will successfully argue against John receiving expectancy damages because the one-million dollar prize and lost profits are too speculative. Here, although John thinks he has a good chance of winning the prize if he submits the painting he will purchase from Bill, it is not guaranteed. Further, courts are hesitant to award a plaintiff lost profits. Again, although John believes that it will increase circulation of his magazine, it is not guaranteed that winning the contest would increase that circulation and result in above average profits for John's magazine. Therefore, it is unlikely that John will receive expectancy damages.

IV.   Venue

John and Bill entered into a contract. Bill contacted John to tell him that he would be breaching the contract. John is seeking a TRO or, in the alternative, specific performance and damages associated with the breach.

John will argue that he can bring his contract action in either the State or Superior Court. The State Court is a trial court of general civil jurisdiction without regard to the amount in controversy, except as to those matters within the exclusive jurisdiction of the Superior Court. Bill will argue that John can only bring the action in the Superior Court. The Superior Court has exclusive jurisdiction over injunctions.

The Superior Court in the county that has personal jurisdiction over Bill would be in the only court that John could bring this contract action. Here, John is seeking specific performance or damages, but also a TRO and in the alternative a preliminary injunction. If he filed in the state court, they would not be able to grant the injunctive relief he was seeking, only the contract damages.

V.   Relief from Court

John is seeking the following relief: a TRO and/or injunction, specific performance, and in the alternative, expectancy and reliance damages for Bill's breach of contract.

John will argue that he can receive all of the relief he is seeking because of the breach of contract. A plaintiff in a breach of contract action has the ability to seek a TRO or injunction, specific performance, and related damages. Bill will argue that John cannot receive expectancy damages. Damages cannot be speculative.

John will most likely receive a TRO to stop the immediate harm of losing the rare painting if Bill is allowed to ship the painting within the week to Frenchie, a bona fide purchaser. The rarity of the painting is also his best argument to be awarded specific performance of the contact. Further, John will also likely receive reliance damages in the amount of $10,000 (nonrefundable fee from contest) if he does not receive the painting from Bill. If the case goes to trial, he may also be able to seek reasonable attorneys fees and costs.

FEBRUARY 2017 BAR EXAMINATION

QUESTION #1   Tort Remedies / Prof. Resp.

On the morning of the day on which this collision occurred, Driver 1, accompanied by his friend, Passenger, drove a small Toyota pickup truck from his home in Hawkinsville to a farm implement auction in Moultrie, where Driver 1 purchased a heavy piece of farm equipment. Employees of the auction company loaded the piece of farm equipment onto a small flatbed trailer which Driver 1 was towing behind his pickup truck. Driver 1 assisted in the loading operation and helped the auction company employees lash the equipment to the trailer. The weight of this equipment was greater than the manufacturer recommended for this trailer, and the combined weight of the equipment and trailer was greater than the towing capacity of the pickup truck, according to its manufacturer.

As they watched the balance of the farm auction and visited with friends, Driver 1 and Passenger began to drink beer they brought with them. After the close of the auction, and the consumption of a great quantity of beer, Driver 1 and Passenger began the return trip to Hawkinsville in the pickup truck with the attached trailer and farm equipment. At a point between Cordele and Abbeville, the pickup truck topped a small hill and Driver 1 saw a car, which was driven by Driver 2, backing out of a driveway into his lane of the two-lane highway. At the same time, and approaching the pickup truck from the opposite direction, was a car being operated by Driver 3, a nurse, who was driving to the hospital in Cordele where she was to begin working the evening shift.

When he saw Driver 2 back into his lane, Driver 1 slammed on the brakes of the pickup truck, causing the farm equipment to shift forward over the tongue of the trailer. As a result, the front of the trailer, with the added weight, went down toward the pavement, forcing the rear of the pickup truck toward the pavement as well, and raising the front tires of the pickup off the pavement. As a consequence, Driver 1 was unable to steer the pickup truck at all. As the pickup truck went out of control, the trailer and farm implement swung across the center line of the roadway and collided with Driver 3's vehicle as she approached, despite the fact that Driver 3 was exercising ordinary care at all times.

As a result of the collision between the trailer and farm equipment hitting Driver 3's vehicle, Driver 3 received catastrophic injuries which were permanently disabling. Driver 1 managed to avoid any significant injury. However, Passenger was thrown from the pickup truck and died as a result of his injuries. Driver 2 did not receive any injury; and in fact, Driver 2 pulled back into his driveway immediately upon seeing the pickup truck top the hill approaching his driveway.

After the collision, it was determined by the investigating law enforcement officers that Driver 1 was under the influence of alcohol to an extent greater than the legal limit.

Considering the facts stated above, please respond to the following questions:

Questions:

1. Driver 3 was married, had two young children, and was employed at the hospital in Cordele. Passenger was a single, unemployed adult with no children who lived with his parents. If lawsuits were filed to seek damages due to the injuries suffered by Driver 3, and due to the death of Passenger, what types of damages might be sought as to each, by whom, and against whom?

2. Please discuss the affirmative defenses that might be available to rebut the various claims for damages sought on behalf of Driver 3 and due to Passenger's death.

3. During the course of the litigation which was initiated by Driver 3, Driver 3 signed an agreement presented to her by a physician pursuant to which Driver 3 pledged to pay her doctor's fees from her future recovery of damages. The case ultimately settled before trial and, despite her lawyer's efforts to address the issue of the outstanding medical expenses, Driver 3 refused to let her lawyer negotiate or tender any payment on her behalf to the doctor, saying that she "would look after the doctor". The doctor insisted upon payment and Driver 3 refused to authorize her lawyer to make the payment. What should Driver 3's lawyer do and why?

QUESTION #2 Buisness Orgs.

Mr. Cash has developed opportunities, both domestically and abroad, to build warehouse facilities that utilize solar energy for power. Because of the popularity of and cost-savings associated with the use of solar energy, Mr. Cash already has many investors who would like to invest in his ventures. In connection with his warehouse business, Mr. Cash would like to set up an entity that will allow for investment by these and other investors. Additionally, this entity must be one in which profits can be retained so that the entity can acquire other businesses in the future to augment the current business model.

Mr. Cash also would like to create an entity that will be owned by Mr. Cash and two of his friends, each of whom will contribute the initial capital to the business. This business entity will manufacture and sell solar panels both for his warehouse facilities and for other commercial and residential users. Instead of retaining the profits from the sales in this entity, Mr. Cash wants to distribute all the profits it makes to the investors in the business. At the same time, he would like to protect the three investors in this company from potential liability that could arise out of their involvement in the business.

Finally, because he is socially conscious, Mr. Cash also would like to set up an entity in honor of his grandmother. He would like to use some of the profits from his business ventures to provide funds through this entity to organizations that promote humanitarian causes and provide education, healthcare and other social services to impoverished communities. He has friends who would like to donate funds to such an entity, but they are only willing to donate if their contributions are tax-exempt.

Mr. Cash knows there are various types of entities that can be used for differing purposes, and he seeks your advice on the types of entities that should be created in order to accomplish his goals.

Questions:
1. Applying Georgia law, what type of entity should Mr. Cash organize that will allow investors to invest in the entity and allow that entity to retain profits for investment in future business opportunities? Explain fully and include in your answer a discussion of the steps and procedures Mr. Cash will be required to follow to legally create and register in the State of Georgia the entity you recommend.
2. Applying Georgia law, what type of entity should Mr. Cash organize that will allow for the manufacture and sale of solar panels and the distribution of the profits from the sales to the investors in the business? Explain how this entity is created and the benefits of its use.
3. Finally, applying Georgia law, what type of entity should Mr. Cash organize that can accept donations to be used for the public good that will not create tax consequences for individual donors? Explain how this entity is created.

QUESTION #3 · Constitutional Law

The State of Georgia has enacted a law creating a tuition voucher program which allows any student in kindergarten through 8th grade who is currently enrolled in a failing public school system under state control to receive a tuition voucher to partially offset the cost of attending another participating public or private school. While less than 20 percent of eligible students have taken advantage of the tuition voucher program, of those who have, more than 90 percent use the vouchers to enroll in Catholic school.

Due to an increasing number of drunken driving incidents, the City of Savannah enacted an ordinance banning the consumption of alcohol within the city limits. The ordinance has no exceptions. Savannah Church has been located within the city limits for more than 50 years. Consumption of alcohol is an important part of the Savannah Church communion service. Because of the ordinance, Savannah Church is not allowed to hold services that include the consumption of alcohol within the city limits.

The City of Tybee Island has enacted an ordinance banning the consumption of alcohol in a designated area of the city that has been the site of several drunken driving incidents. The only building located in the area subject to the alcohol ban is Tybee Church, which is the only church in the City of Tybee. Tybee Church also considers consumption of alcohol an important part of the Tybee Church communion service. In addition to having church services in the building, Tybee Church also has wedding receptions and other events in the church building during which alcohol is consumed. Because of the ordinance, Tybee Church is effectively prohibited from holding communion services that include consumption of alcohol on church property.

The Georgia state law and the City of Savannah and City of Tybee ordinances have been challenged as violating the First Amendment of the United States Constitution by parties who have standing to challenge the law and the ordinances.

Questions:
1. How will the Court likely rule on the challenge to the State of Georgia law on the school voucher program? Explain your answer fully.
2. How will the Court likely rule on the challenge to the City of Savannah ordinance? Explain your answer fully.
3. How will the Court likely rule on the challenge to the City of Tybee ordinance? Explain your answer fully.

QUESTION #4   Trusts

Grandpa Jones had only one son, Jeff, who died in a tragic automobile accident in 2003. Jeff was married to Martha, and had two young children, Rob, born in 1997, and Justine, born in 2000.

After Jeff's unexpected death, Grandpa decided he needed to create a trust fund for Rob and Justine to pay for their ongoing support, college education and health care expenses. Because Martha had very limited income, Grandpa felt the need to supplement the financial support which Martha would provide her children.

Grandpa selected two of Jeff's closest friends, Bill and Hank, to be trustees of the trust for his grandchildren. To fund the trust, Grandpa decided to transfer to Bill and Hank, as trustees, a 50-acre tract of raw land which Grandpa had owned for many years, located about one-half of a mile from I-85 north of Atlanta. While the land had limited value on the date the trust was created, Grandpa felt it would appreciate in value over time and provide his grandchildren with more than adequate financial support.

Grandpa created the trust in 2005, but in 2015, after Rob had turned 18 years of age and was about to enter college, Bill and Hank, as trustees, realized that the 50-acre tract held in the trust was producing no income and would not provide any financial support for Rob to pay tuition, room and board and travel expenses during his college years. Because there was a limited market for the 50-acre tract held in the trust, Bill suggested to Hank that he, meaning Bill, would be willing to purchase the tract from the trust at its current fair market value, thus exchanging the tract for cash which could be invested and which could provide Rob with the financial support he would need during his college years. The trust fund would also be available to help Justine when she reached college age.

Bill proceeded to have the tract appraised by a qualified MAI appraiser who determined the tract to be valued at $2,000 per acre. Hank wondered if Bill's purchase of the tract was a good idea, but did not object to the transaction. Bill also told Martha of his plan; Martha too agreed that this would be in her children's best interest. Bill proceeded to purchase the tract from the trust for $100,000 cash in 2015.

In September 2016, Moxie Industries, an international plastics conglomerate, decided to move its headquarters to Georgia and wanted to find a suitable location for its production facility and corporate offices. Grandpa's 50-acre tract, which Bill now owned, turned out to be the perfect location for Moxie, and it offered Bill $10,000 per acre for the land, which Bill quickly accepted. The transaction closed in February 2017, and Bill was paid $500,000 for the tract.

Rob is now 19 years of age, while Justine is 16. Please address the following questions as you analyze these facts:

Questions:
1. Has Bill or Hank breached any fiduciary duty which either of them may have had to Rob and Justine under applicable Georgia law? If so, describe how either or both of them may have breached a duty to Rob and Justine. Please discuss or explain your answer fully.
2. If you conclude that Bill or Hank or both are liable to Rob and Justine in connection with the described transactions, are they equally liable according to applicable Georgia law, or does one co-trustee have greater liability than the other? Please discuss or explain your answer fully.
3. If Rob and Justine wish to file a lawsuit against Bill, Hank or both under applicable Georgia law, how long will each of them have to file such a suit?
4. What legal remedy should Rob and Justine seek? Please discuss or explain your answer fully.
5. Finally, under applicable Georgia law, was there a judicial remedy available to Bill and Hank, as trustees, which would have allowed them to sell the tract to Bill without creating the potential for a claim or claims to be made against them by the grandchildren? Please discuss or explain your answer fully.

FEBRUARY 2017 BAR EXAMINATION ANSWERS

MODEL ANSWER TO QUESTION #1

1. Damages that could be claimed:

Driver Three v. Driver One

Driver Three was a nurse who was employed by the hospital in Cordele. She was on her way to work and exhibited ordinary care while operating her vehicle when Driver One's truck went out of control and collided with her vehicle. Driver Three was married with two young children and suffered catastrophic injuries that were permanently disabling.

Driver three will argue she can seek compensatory damages against Driver One for loss of wages, loss of consortium, and pain and suffering. A plaintiff can seek compensatory damages, that is, damages that are foreseeable, when monetary relief can make the plaintiff whole or as close to whole as possible before the incident occurred. Drive One will argue however that he was not responsible for Driver Three's injures because it was not foreseeable that the trailer would cause the pickup truck to be uncontrollable.

Driver Three will win her claim for compensatory damages against Driver One because his negligence caused the accident, which resulted in physical harm to her. Driver One failed to exercise ordinary care due to the fact that the trailer was overloaded. Furthermore, Driver One was under the influence of alcohol, which would therefore suggest he was in fact negligent in transporting the farm equipment under the circumstances. As a result of the accident, Driver Three suffered severe injuries, which rendered her incapable of working. Based on Driver One' actions, it was foreseeable that an accident would have occurred. Therefore, Driver Three is owed compensatory damages for her injuries.

Driver Three's Spouse and Children v. Driver One

Driver Three was severely injured in an accident, which occurred as a result of Driver One attempting to swerve from a potential collision with Driver Two. Driver One was carrying excess weight in the trailer being driven and was drunk.

Driver Three's family could argue that they are entitled to economic damages (that is, loss of income) for Driver One's negligence as the ensuing accident was foreseeable and Driver One should have known that it was likely that her husband and children would suffer damages as a result of his tortious acts. A duty of care is owed to take reasonable measures to avoid the risk of causing economic damages, apart from physical injury, to plaintiffs of an identifiable class, where the defendant knows or has reason to know that they are likely to suffer such a damage. Driver One would argue that he does not know Driver Three nor whether she had a family or not, therefore her family (or class of people) are not foreseeable parties who can sue for compensatory damages. Plaintiffs must be particularly foreseeable, their presence foreseeable, the number of the class predictable, and the economic expectations sure.

Driver Three's family would prevail in their claim against Driver One for economic damages as a result of his negligence because Driver One knew or had reason to know that Driver Three would have a family, as a class of people, who he knew would have suffered damages as a result of his negligent acts. It is not farfetched that Driver Three would have a family, therefore it would be difficult for Driver One to argue that his conduct in overloading his van and trailer and driving while under the influence would not have severe repercussions if he caused an accident resulting in severe injuries to another, like Driver Three.

Damages that can be claimed by Passenger

Passenger accompanied Driver One to a farm implement auction in on the day of the collision. During the collision passenger was thrown from the pickup truck and died as a result of his injuries. Passenger was a single unemployed adult with no children, who lived with his parents.

Passenger's estate (his parents) will argue that Driver One is responsible for providing compensatory damages and punitive damages. Compensatory damages are monetary in nature and are used to make the plaintiff whole for the losses sustained. Punitive damages serve to punish the defendant for egregious conduct and to stop other possible defendants from engaging in similar behavior. Driver One will argue that Passenger assumed the risk because he knowingly got in the car with an intoxicated driver and thus knowingly consented to any risk that occurred. In Georgia, there is no guest statute. Therefore, a driver owes only a duty of ordinary care to someone in the car with them.

Passenger's Estate will lose on the punitive damages claim because Driver

One's conduct was not malicious; he tried to prevent an accident occurring when Driver Two started backing out. To be held liable for punitive damages the conduct must be of such that the defendant's behavior is malicious, wanton, or willful to warrant punitive damages. Although driver overloaded his truck with the equipment and drove under the influence of alcohol, he tried to avoid the accident by swerving out of Driver Two's way. He is thus not guilty of malicious or wanton conduct to warrant the grant of punitive damages. Passenger's Estate will however win a claim for compensatory damages because Driver One did not exhibit ordinary care in his driving when he made the decision to operate an overloaded vehicle while intoxicated. Therefore, Driver One will owe compensatory damages to Passenger's Estate.

2. Affirmative Defenses of Driver One against Driver Three

Driver Three was a nurse who was employed by the hospital in Cordele. She was on her way to work when Driver One's truck got out of control and collided with her vehicle. Driver Three suffered catastrophic injuries which were permanently disabling.

Driver One would argue that Driver Three assumed the risk of being involved in an accident of this sort by voluntarily driving on the roadway, therefore Driver Three is completely barred from recovery. The assumption of risk may be implied if the plaintiff knew of the risk and voluntarily consented to take it on nonetheless. Driver Three would argue that she did not actually know that Driver One would have driven his overloaded truck on the roadway while drunk, nor that Driver Two would attempt to back out of his driveway in a negligent manner. The risk must be actually known to the Plaintiff.

Driver Three would prevail in her argument that she had no actual knowledge of the facts leading up to the accident, therefore she cannot be charged with assuming the risk of this accident by driving on the road on this occasion.

Affirmative Defenses of Driver One against Passenger

Passenger accompanied Driver One to a farm implement auction in on the day of the collision. During the collision passenger was thrown from the pickup truck and died as a result of his injuries.

Driver One would argue that Passenger did not take reasonable care to protect his own safety as he willingly went with him to collect the equipment and he too willingly drove back with him in an overloaded truck, while they were both drunk, thus he is therefore contributory negligent. A plaintiff will be found contributory negligent if his actions contribute proximately to his injuries. Passenger's estate will argue that Passenger's act in agreeing to join him on the trip back with the overburdened truck while intoxicated is not the proximate cause of his death, but that of Driver One's and Driver Two's actions. Plaintiff's negligence must be proximately and actually connected to his injuries.

Driver One would prevail in his argument that Passenger was contributory negligent in causing his death because Passenger willingly and knowingly joined Driver One in driving with him in the overburdened truck, while they were both intoxicated. Here, Passenger would be charged with the same standard of care as Driver One in ensuring his safety whilst driving with him. Passenger knowingly boarded the truck when the truck was overloaded and they both drank until they were drunk and he willingly accepted the risk of Driver One operating the vehicle while under the influence. Thus Passenger willingly placed himself in the position of unreasonable danger, and he therefore assumed the risk associated with it.

3. Third Party Creditor Claim

Driver Three signed an agreement presented to her by her physician pledging her to pay doctor's fees from her future award of damages. The case has settled and Driver Three was awarded money. The doctor is insists on payment and Driver Three has refused to authorize her attorney to make the payment.

The Lawyer will argue that he is duty bound to set aside the fees owed to the doctor because there is a valid claim from a creditor that is in dispute. Under the Georgia Professional Code of Conduct the attorney is a custodian of client property and has a duty to protect a third party's claim against wrongful interference by the client. Client will argue that the attorney should not pay the doctor because he does not have a duty to anyone but her.

The attorney would prevail in his argument because he is duty bound by the Professional Code of Conduct set aside the fees in dispute until all issues are resolved. Attorney is therefore bound to keep the disputed funds in the client's trust account until all disputes between the third party and the doctor have been addressed. However, Attorney can pay Driver Three the funds which are owed to her and not in dispute.

MODEL ANSWER TO QUESTION #2

A. Type of Entity Created Under Georgia Law

Mr. Cash built warehouse facilities that utilize solar energy for power. Many investors would like to invest in Mr. Cash's ventures. Mr. Cash is interested in setting up an entity that will allow for investment by these and other investors so that it would be able to retain profits to acquire other businesses in the future to augment the current business model.

Mr. Cash would argue that the proper entity to be organized would be to create a closed corporation or C. Corp. as this kind of entity would allow profits to be retained by the corporation which would then be reinvested differently. Under Georgia Law a closed corporation may be used to facilitate business ventures for the purposes of expansion and venture capital funding. Investors would argue that the articles of corporation and bylaws cannot be so drafted to incorporate the objective of Mr. Cash in using the profits for solar energy power expansion to reinvest differently.

Mr. Cash would prevail in his argument that a closed corporation would be a viable option in retaining its profits to acquire other similar business, so long as it is in conformity with its Articles of Incorporation and bylaws. To create this entity Mr. Cash will need to have a meeting with the investors to draft and adopt the by-laws and the articles of incorporation. Once the articles of incorporation are created and approved they need to be submitted to the Secretary of State. The Entity becomes a C Corporation once the Secretary of State files the articles of incorporation.

B. Creating a Corporation in Georgia

Mr. Cash wants to create an entity for its manufacturing business and he has two friends who are willing to contribute the initial capital of the business. They want to allow for the manufacturing and sale of solar panels and the distribution of profits from the sales to the investors in the business. Mr. Cash also wants to protect the investors from potential liability that could arise out of their involvement in the business.

Mr. Cash would argue that the proper entity to be organized is a limited liability corporation, as it will allow for complete protection of his investors of the business to the extent of their contributions, and the entity will allow for profit sharing among its investors. Under Georgia law, a limited liability corporation is an entity that has limited liability for the owners, while allowing for profit sharing among its investors, so long as this objective accords with its articles of incorporation and bylaws. The investors would argue that a partnership is more befitting since it will allow for capital sharing among its investors and it need not be formally created. A partnership may be implied rather than formally created.

Mr. Cash would also prevail in this argument since a corporation would provide limited liability of his investors for potential liability that may arise from the involvement of business, while it may provide for profit sharing among its investors or directors. Even though a partnership would allow for profit sharing among the partners, the partnership would not be a viable option in safeguarding from potential liability as each partner would be jointly and severally liable for any potential liability that may arise from the venture. This type of entity is created by filing its articles of organization with the Secretary of State. The benefits of this organization are that there is centralized management and the investors have limited liability for debts and other liabilities.

C. Creating a nonprofit in Georgia

Mr. Cash is trying to organize an entity that can accept donations to be used for the public good that will not create tax consequences for individual donors.

Mr. Cash would argue that he could create such a vehicle through incorporating a nonprofit corporation. Under Georgia law a nonprofit organization is created for solely charitable purposes. The investors would argue however that a limited liability corporation could be established for charitable purpose.

Mr. Cash would again prevail in his argument, since a nonprofit corporation can be utilized for the very purpose of operating a charitable organization, and due to its charitable nature, its contributions are also tax-exempt. To create such an entity the articles of incorporation must be filed with the Secretary of State, which should explicitly state that a nonprofit corporation is being created. Then a publication of notice of intent to file of articles of incorporation should be completed as well.

MODEL ANSWER TO QUESTION #3

A. School Voucher Program

The State of Georgia has a tuition voucher program which allows that any student in kindergarten through 8th grade currently enrolled in a failing public school system under state control can use the vouchers to partially offset the costs of attending another participating school. Less than 20% of eligible students used the voucher and 90% of the tuition vouchers are being used at Catholic school.

The Plaintiff will argue that the State of Georgia has violated the First Amendment of the United States Constitution because the tuition voucher program supports the Catholic Church. The First Amendment prohibits Congress and the states (through the Fourteenth Amendment) from respecting an establishment of religion. The State of Georgia will argue that the tuition voucher program does not violate the First Amendment because the issuance of the voucher was for the secular purpose, that of promoting better means of education of students among failing schools, it has no control over what school is selected by these students and there is no entanglement with the Catholic school. Under the First Amendment, a similar law can be enacted as long as it is neutral and general with only an incidental burden on religion.

The State of Georgia would prevail in its argument that it has not breached the provisions of the First Amendment, since the voucher system implemented was for a secular purpose of enhancing the ability of students to achieve better education and there was no entanglement with the Catholic Church. The test to determine if the government has established a religion is based on whether the purpose of the law enacted had a secular reason, does not have a principal or primary effect that advances one religion over another, and the law must not foster excessive governmental entanglement with religion. Here, the State sought to assist students in failing public schools by providing vouchers to offset some of the expenses in attending other schools. The State has no control over what the vouchers were used for, nor the kind of schools chosen by the recipients. The fact that Catholic schools were chosen over others does not show that the state has become entangled in religion since its purpose was a secular one.

B. City of Savannah Ordinance

The City of Savannah enacted an ordinance banning the consumption of alcohol within city limits without exceptions. The city ordinance was enacted to lower the number of drunken driving incidents. A Savannah church located within the city limits consumes alcohol during their communion service and is now prohibited from doing so because of the city ordinance.

The Savannah church will argue that the city ordinance violates their First Amendment right to practice their religious belief because it prohibits the members from consuming alcohol during their communion services. Under the First Amendment, no government body may abridge the rights of any citizen from practicing their religious beliefs. The City of Savannah will argue however, that the ordinance does not violate any rights because it is prohibiting the consumption of alcohol due to the increase in the number of drunken driving incidents, and is thus justified by a compelling state need. The state may regulate or punish an activity practiced by a religion if it is justified by a compelling state need. Savannah Church will argue that the ordinance is still a violation of their First Amendment rights because the ordinance has more than an incidental burden on religion and the City of Savannah can find other means to keep the incidence of drunk driving down.

A court will likely find that the City of Savannah's ordinance is constitutional because the ordinance does not abridge the Church of Savannah's freedom to practice their religious belief. Here, the facts are that the ordinance was enacted to quell the rise in incidence of drunk driving, which is arguably a compelling state need. The City is therefore obliged to prohibit or control alcohol consumption within the affected area. The church was coincidentally within the city limits and will thus be affected by the ordinance. The church's inability to consume alcohol during their communion service does not stop them from practicing their religious belief therefore the ordinance is constitutional.

C. City of Tybee Ordinance

The City of Tybee Island has enacted an ordinance banning the consumption of alcohol in a designated area of the city that has been the site of several drunken driving incidents. Tybee Church is located in the area that is subject to the alcohol ban. Tybee church considers consumption of alcohol an important part of their communion service. Tybee Church also has wedding receptions and other events in the church building during which alcohol is consumed.

Tybee Church will argue that the ordinance is unconstitutional because the ordinance only affects their building and it interferes with their religious practice of consuming alcohol, which is important to their religious practices. The City of Tybee Island will argue however that the ordinance is constitutional because the purpose of enacting the ban of alcoholic consumption within the area was due to the incidence of drunken driving, and therefore serves a compelling state need. The state may regulate or punish an activity practiced by a religion if it is justified by a compelling state need.

The Court will likely rule that the City of Tybee Island ordinance is constitutional because it only prohibits the consumption of alcohol in a designated area. The ordinance also does not prohibit the Tybee Church from practicing their religious belief. The incidence of drunk driving in an area is a compelling state need on the part of the City to enact laws to prohibit or to control alcohol consumption for public safety reason. In balancing the interests of the church in continuing its alcoholic consumption and the City in protecting its citizens from the effect of drunk driving, the court is more likely to hold that the legitimate interest of public safety is more compelling. Therefore, the City of Tybee has not violated the First Amendment.

MODEL ANSWER TO QUESTION #4

1. Fiduciary duties to beneficiaries of Trust

Grandpa Jones created trust fund for his two grandchildren, Justine and Rob, to pay for their ongoing support, college education, and health care expenses. He selected Bill and Hank as trustees of the trust for his grandchildren. The trust holds a 50- acre tract of raw land. Bill bought the 50-acre tract at fair market value for $100,000 after getting the tract appraised by an independent third party and speaking with the beneficiaries' mother. A year later Moxie Industries purchased the same tract of land from Bill for $500,000. Rob was 18 at the time the tract was bought by Bill.

Justin and Rob would argue that Bill and Hank breached their duty of loyalty and good faith because they sold the trust property to one trustee without consulting a court or Rob. A trustee has a duty of loyalty and good faith in their role as the fiduciary of a trust and must avoid any conflict between his own interest and that of the trust. Bill and Hank would argue however, that they acted in good faith because the land was not producing income to sustain the children and when they decided that

Bill would purchase the land they hired an independent land appraiser to give them its fair market value. A trustee has the duty to make a property productive and the prudent man rule is used to determine what is the most suitable step to take in preserving and maximizing trust property for the sole benefit of the beneficiaries.

A court will likely determine that Bill and Hank breached their duty of good faith and loyalty to the beneficiaries because Bill self-dealt when purchasing the land and Hank allowed it. Furthermore, Bill should have consulted the Rob, who was now an adult, and the courts (since Justine was still a minor) before purchasing the land even if he hired an independent appraiser and bought the land at fair market value. A trustee must avoid all impressions of impropriety. The trustee cannot self-deal unless he has permission in the trust documents or permission from the courts or consent from the adult beneficiaries who are knowledgeable of the details of the transaction. The trustees therefore breached their fiduciary duty under the trust and are thus liable under the theory of constructive trust.

2. Liability of Trustees

Bill and Hank realized that the 50-acre tract held in the trust was producing no income and would not provide any financial support for Rob to pay tuition, room and board, and travel expenses during his college years. Bill and Hank discussed Bill purchasing the land at fair market value. Bill had the tract appraised by an MAI appraiser. Hank had some reservations about purchasing the land but did not openly object to the purchase. A year later Moxie Industries offered to Bill, the new owner of the tract, $500,000 to purchase it. Bill sold it to them.

Justine and Rob would argue that Bob and Hank are equally liable to them because they are co-trustees and have to act in accord as one, especially in the sale of land where they are both listed on the deed and must both execute documents to effect the sale. If there are co-trustees then they must act as one unless the trust instrument states otherwise. Bill and Hank will argue however that they are not both liable because only one of them actually purchased the land.

A court will find that both trustees are equally liable because they are co-trustees and the trust document does not give them the power to act independently of each other before decision can be made. The trust document controls the powers and duties of the trustee. This document also can establish more than one trustee. Under trust administration the co-trustees must act together and in one accord so that any decisions made are made with both approvals, not just one. Here, Rob decided to purchase the land and although Hank had reservations, he agreed nonetheless and the sale was effected. Therefore, both trustees would be liable for the dissipation of trust assets.

3. Lawsuit against Trustees

Bill and Hank agreed for Bob to purchase the trust property for $100,000 in

2015. One year later, Bill sold the land for $500,000.

Rob will argue that he has six years and Justine will argue that she has six years after she reaches the age of majority to file a lawsuit against the trustees once they have discovered the breach. Under Georgia Trust Code the beneficiaries have six years (provided that all beneficiaries attain the age of majority) to file a suit for a breach of fiduciary duty against the trustee. Bill and Hank would argue however that the claim is not actionable since Justine has not attained the age of majority.

Rob and Justine would prevail as the Statue of Limitations provides that a breach of this nature is actionable within six years of the discovery of the breach. Furthermore, the statute of limitation will not begin to run against Justine until she attains the age of majority, while Rob has an actionable claim upon discovery of the trustees' breach.

4. Legal Remedy

Bill and Hank agreed for Bob to purchase the trust property for $100,000 in 2015. One year later, Bill sold the land for $500,000. Bill did not seek permission from the beneficiaries for the purchase of the property.

Rob and Justine would argue that they are entitled to damages under the theory of a constructive trust by the court for the purchase price of the land sale between Bill and Moxie Industries because of their breach of their fiduciary duty as a trustee. Under Georgia law, a beneficiary can seek an equitable remedy for breach of fiduciary duties under the theory of a constructive trust which is an equitable remedy that is created by the court to make the beneficiaries whole when the trustee has breached their duty and has benefitted wrongfully from trust assets. Bill and Hank would argue that there is no equitable or legal remedy available because the land was purchased at fair market value at the time of the sale for the benefit of the Beneficiaries.

A court will likely to find that a constructive trust was created in the proceeds of sale by Bill for the beneficiaries and will order that the funds obtained from the sale be returned to the trust because the trustees breached their fiduciary duty when they sold the property to themselves without consulting the court and the beneficiaries. This is an egregious breach of a relationship based on trust. Therefore, in order to achieve equity, the Court will order that the $500,000 be paid over to the trust.

5. Judicial Remedy available to Trustees

Bill and Hank agreed for Bob to purchase the trust property for $100,000 in 2015. One year later, Bill sold the land for $500,000. Bill did not seek permission from the beneficiaries for the purchase of the property.

Bill and Hank would argue that they could have petitioned the court as the trustees to dissolve the trust since prior to its sale to Bill, the land was practically useless to benefit the beneficiaries in accordance with the provisions of the trust. Trustees have the power to petition the court to have the terms of the trust restructured or dissolved on the basis that the trust is not providing the benefit to the beneficiaries as envisioned by the trust instrument. Justine and Rob would argue on the other hand that they would be entitled to defend such a claim on the basis that the objectives of the trust are not worthless, and no provision was made in the trust instrument for any petition for reconstruction or dissolution to be made by the trustees.

Bill and Hank should have sought the court's permission regarding selling the property because it was not explicitly stated as a power they had in the trust. Under Georgia trust code a trust document gives explicit powers to the trustee and anything outside of those powers is not allowed. The trustee can however seek the permission of the court, if there is a need so to do, to administer the trust in ways not explicitly stated in the trust instrument. When a court grants permission, it as if the powers were written in the trust and the beneficiaries have to go along with that decision.

Made in the USA
Columbia, SC
24 May 2018